The Ultimate Lateral & Critical Thinking Puzzle Book

The Ultimate Lateral & Critical Thinking Puzzle Book

By Paul Sloane, Des MacHale
& Michael A. DiSpezio

Sterling Publishing Co., Inc.
New York

10 9 8 7 6 5 4 3 2 1

Published by Sterling Publishing Co., Inc.
387 Park Avenue South, New York, NY 10016
This book is comprised of the following Sterling titles:
Ingenious Lateral Thinking Puzzles©1998 by Paul Sloane and Des MacHale
Tricky Lateral Thinking Puzzles©1999 by Paul Sloane and Des MacHale
Super Lateral Thinking Puzzles©2000 by Paul Sloane and Des MacHale
Critical Thinking Puzzles©1996 by Michael A. DiSpezio
Great Critical Thinking Puzzles©1997 by Michael A. DiSpezio
Challenging Critical Thinking Puzzles©1998 by Michael A. DiSpezio
All illustrated by Myron Miller

© 2002 by Sterling Publishing Co., Inc.
Distributed in Canada by Sterling Publishing
c/o Canadian Manda Group, One Atlantic Avenue, Suite 105
Toronto, Ontario, Canada M6K 3E7
Distributed in Great Britain and Europe by Chrysalis Books
64 Brewery Road, London N7 9NT, England
Distributed in Australia by Capricorn Link (Australia) Pty. Ltd.
P.O. Box 704, Windsor, NSW 2756, Australia

Printed in China

Sterling 1-4027-0307-4

Contents

Lateral Thinking Puzzles

Critical Thinking Puzzles

Lateral Thinking Puzzles

A man was held in a high-security prison and closely watched. His wife sent him a letter in which she was asked, "Should I plant the potatoes in the garden now?" He replied, "Do not plant anything in the garden. That is where I hide the guns." A little later he received another letter from his wife saying, "Many policemen came to our house. They dug up the whole garden but they did not find anything." He wrote back, "Now is the time to plant the potatoes."

That man used a little lateral thinking to solve his wife's gardening problem—and so can we all. We need new and creative ways of problem-solving, and more and more people see lateral thinking puzzles as a way to fire up this process. Trainers use these puzzles in management training courses to force managers to check their assumptions; teachers use them in class to stimulate and reward children; parents use them on long journeys to amuse and challenge the family. In all cases, the procedure is similar. One person knows the answer and he or she answers the questions from the other players.

The puzzles in this section are situation puzzles. They should be fun—but they also help to develop skills in questioning, deduction, logic, and lateral thinking. They are based in a statement of a situation that you have to use as a starting point in order to arrive at a particular explanation or solution. Often there can be many possible scenarios that explain the puzzle, but you have to find the "right" answer.

It is better to do these puzzles in a small group rather than try to solve them individually. Typically they contain insufficient information for you to immediately deduce the solution. You need to ask questions in order to gather more information before you can formulate solutions.

One person acts as quizmaster. He or she reads the puzzle aloud and reads the solution silently. The others ask questions in order to gather information, check assumptions, and test solutions. The quizmaster can answer in one of four ways: "Yes," "No," "Irrelevant," or "Please rephrase the question."

If people get stuck, the quizmaster can offer one or more of the clues in the Clues section. The aim is to arrive at the solution given in the Answer section, not simply to find a situation that satisfies the initial conditions.

As with most problems we face, it is best to start by testing your assumptions, and by asking broad questions that establish general conditions, motives, and actions. Don't narrow in on specific solutions until you have first established the broad parameters of what is going on.

When you get stuck, attack the problem from a new direction—think laterally!

Lateral Thinking Puzzles

The Tracks of My Tires

The police found a murder victim and they noticed a pair of tire tracks leading to and from the body. They followed the tracks to a nearby farmhouse where two men and a woman were sitting on the porch. There was no car at the farmhouse and none of the three could drive. The police arrested the woman. Why?

Clues: 212/Answer: 249.

▽◁▲▽◁▲▽◁▲▽◁▲▽◁

Bertha's Travels

Every day Bertha travels 30 miles in the course of her work. She doesn't travel in a wheeled vehicle and never has problems with traffic, the police, weather, or airports. What does she do?

Clues: 203/Answer: 241.

▽◁▲▽◁▲▽◁▲▽◁▲▽◁

The Upset Woman

When the woman saw him she was upset. Even though she had never seen him before, she had left some food for him because she knew he would be hungry. But he could not reach the food because he had an iron bar across his back. He died soon after and the woman was pleased. What's going on?

Clues: 213/Answer: 250.

Sick Leave

Walter spent three days in the hospital. He was neither sick nor injured, but when it was time to leave he had to be carried out. Why?

Clues: 211/Answer: 248.

Top at Last

William was the least intelligent and laziest boy in a class of 30 students who took an examination. Yet when the results were announced, William's name was at the top of the list. How come?

Clues: 212/Answer: 249.

In the Middle of the Night

A man wakes up at night in the pitch dark. He knows that on his bedside table are a razor, a watch, and a glass of water. How can he reach out onto the table and be sure to pick up the watch without touching either the razor or the glass of water?

Clues: 206/Answer: 244.

Criminal Assistance

The police put up notices warning the public about a certain type of crime, but this actually helped the criminals. How?

Clues: 204/Answer: 242.

I'D LIKE TO PROPOSE A TOAST TO OLD WHAT'S HIS NAME!!

HEAR! HEAR!

HEAR! HEAR!

HEAR! HEAR!

Honorable Intent

Six people who do not know each other get together to honor a seventh person unknown to all of them. Why?

Clues: 206/Answer: 244.

Shell Shock

Why do players very rarely win at the "shell game," where they have to say which of three shuffled shells covers a pea?

Clues: 211/Answer: 248.

Wonderful Weather

A ship sank in perfect weather conditions. If the weather had been worse, the ship would probably not have sunk. What happened?

Clues: 214/Answer:251.

Material Witness

In the fabric shop, the curtains are neatly arranged by style. The floral-patterned ones are in a section marked "Floral," the plain ones are in a section marked "Plain," and the striped ones are in a section marked "Striped." But one pair with vertical blue stripes is not in the "Striped" section. Why not?

Clue: 208/Answer: 245.

Denise and Harry

Denise died at sea while Harry died on land. People were pleased that Harry had died and even more pleased that Denise had died. Why?

Clues: 204/Answer: 242.

Mechanical Advantage

A driver had a problem with his car in a remote area miles from the nearest garage. He stopped at a little candy store, where his problem was quickly solved. How?

Clues: 208/Answer: 245.

The Deadly Dresser

A healthy man got dressed and then lay down and died. Why?

Clues: 204/Answer: 242.

Lifesaver

A politician made a speech that saved his life even before he gave the speech. How?

Clues: 208/Answer: 245.

Landlubber

A man sailed single-handed around the world in a small boat. Yet he was always in sight of land. How come?

Clues: 207/Answer: 245.

Unfinished Business

What work can a sculptor never finish?

Clues: 213/Answer: 250.

Another Landlubber

A man went around the world in a ship. Yet he was always in sight of land. How come?

Clues: 203/Answer: 241.

Plane and Simple

A boy who is three feet tall puts a nail into a tree at his exact height. He returns two years later when he has grown by six inches and the tree has grown by twelve inches. How much taller is the nail than the boy?

Clues: 209/Answer: 246.

HONEY, HAVE YOU SEEN MY NAIL GUN?

Jericho

A man was building a house when it collapsed all around him. He wasn't injured or upset, and he calmly started to rebuild it. What was going on?

Clues: 207/Answer: 244.

Superior Knowledge

When the mother superior returned to the convent after a weekend away, she immediately noticed that a man had been there—and that was strictly against the rules. How did she know?

Clues: 212/Answer: 249.

The Engraving

A woman saw an advertisement for a color engraving of Queen Elizabeth II for $1 and bought it. When it arrived, she had no cause for complaint, but she wasn't pleased. Why?

Clues: 205/Answer: 242.

Rush Job

In 1849, a man went to the California gold rush hoping to make his fortune by selling tents to the miners. However, the weather was fine and the miners slept out in the open, so the man could sell no tents. But he made his fortune anyway and his name is famous to this day. How did he become rich and who is he?

Clues: 210/Answer: 247.

Half for Me and Half for You

It is said that Lucrezia Borgia once split an apple in half and shared it with a companion. Within 10 minutes her companion was dead and Lucrezia survived. How come?

Clues: 206/Answer: 243-244.

Who Did It?

A child at school printed something rude on the wall and nobody owned up to doing it. How did the teacher find out who did it?

Clues: 214/Answer: 250.

Lethal Relief

A famine-stricken Third World country was receiving food aid from the West, but this inadvertently led to the deaths of several people. How?

Clues: 207/Answer: 245.

Chop Chop

Why was an ancient, rare, and healthy tree that stood well away from all buildings in the grounds of Cork University condemned to be cut down?

Clues: 203/Answer: 241.

Hot Job

A man held up a bank on a hot day. He was caught later by the police. On a colder day he would probably not have been caught. Why?

Clues: 206/Answer: 244.

Resistance

During the German advance and occupation of France in World War II, how did some French resistance fighters booby-trap rooms in a way that put Germans more at risk than French people?

Clues: 210/Answer: 247.

Invisible Earnings

Nauru, in the South Pacific, has a high income per capita. But its wealth doesn't come from anything it grows, makes, or mines. Where does its wealth come from?

Clues: 207/Answer: 244.

Basket Case

She was responsible for the deaths of many people, yet she was never charged. How come?

Clues: 203/Answer: 241.

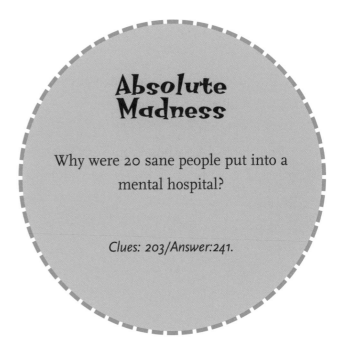

Absolute Madness

Why were 20 sane people put into a mental hospital?

Clues: 203/Answer:241.

WALLY Test I

From the World Association of Learning, Laughter, and Youth (WALLY) comes the WALLY Test! It is a set of quick-fire questions. They may look easy, but be warned—they are designed to trick you. Write down your answers on a piece of paper and then see how many you got right. The time limit is three minutes.

1. If a man bets you that he can bite his eye, should you take the bet?

2. If he now bets you that he can bite his other eye, should you take that bet?

3. How can you stand behind someone while he or she stands behind you?

4. What looks like a horse, moves likes a horse, and is as big as a horse but weighs nothing?

5. Who is bigger: Mr. Bigger or Mr. Bigger's son?

6. Tom's mother had three children. One was named April. One was named May. What was the third one named?

7. Where could you go to see an ancient pyramid, an iceberg, and a huge waterfall?

8. What has four fingers and a thumb but isn't a hand?

9. What multiplies by division?

10. What's white when it's dirty and black when it's clean?

Answers on page 273.

Spies Are Us

During World War I, two German spies often ate at the same restaurant, but they never sat together. How did they pass information?

Clues: 211/Answer: 248.

The Stuffed Cloud

A meteorologist was replaced in his job because of a stuffed cloud. What's a stuffed cloud?

Clues: 212/Answer: 249.

A Strange Collection

At a dinner, a small container is passed around the table and every guest puts something in it. The contents are then thrown away. What's going on?

Clues: 212/Answer: 249.

Tittle Tattle

You have seen many tittles in the last few minutes. What are they?

Clues: 212/Answer: 249.

Outstanding

What feature of *The Old Farmer's Almanac* made it vastly more popular than all its rivals for over 100 years in the rural U.S.?

Clues: 209/Answer: 246.

Foreign Cure

Why does an American fly to another country in the hope of finding a cure for his illness?

Clues: 205/Answer: 243.

Bus Lane Bonus

A city introduced bus lanes on busy streets and the death rate dropped quickly. Why?

Clues: 203/Answer: 241.

Blow by Blow

Why was a man at a fairground blowing darts through a concealed blowpipe?

Clues: 203/Answer: 241.

Paper Tiger

A man writes the same number, and nothing else, on 20 sheets of paper. Why?

Clues: 209/Answer: 246.

▽◁▲▽◁▲▽◁▲▽◁▲▽◁▲▽◁▲▽◁

History Question

What happened in London on September 8, 1752?

Clues: 206/Answer: 244.

▽◁▲▽◁▲▽◁▲▽◁▲▽◁▲▽◁▲▽◁

Forging Ahead

A forger went into a store with a genuine $50 bill. How did he use this to come out with a $20 profit?

Clues: 205/Answer: 243.

Sign Here

A man bought two identical signs but found that he could use only one of them. Why?

Clues: 211/Answer: 248.

Smile Please!

A man wrote to a toothpaste company suggesting a way in which they could significantly increase their sales. How?

Clues: 211/Answer: 248.

High on a Hill

A man was marooned overnight on a mountain above the snow line in winter. He had no protective clothing and no tent. How did he survive?

Clues: 206/Answer: 244.

Mine Shafted

In order to sell it, a con man salted a useless mine with a number of genuine pieces of silver. How did the buyer figure out the scheme?

Clues: 208/Answer: 245.

A Geography Question

Which states of the U.S. are the most western, most southern, most northern, and most eastern?

Clues: 206/Answer: 243.

That Will Teach You

One day a man came home to collect something he had forgotten, and found that his house had been completely destroyed. What had happened?

Clues: 212/Answer: 249.

The Generous General

A retired English general was saddened to see a beggar on the street with a sign reading "World War II veteran." So he gave him £10. The man thanked him and the general became angry. Why?

Clues: 206/Answer: 243.

Fast Mover!

How did a man with an out-of-date passport legitimately visit 30 different countries in the same day?

Clues: 205/Answer: 243.

Running on Empty

Mrs. Jones was very pleased that the car ran out of gas. Why?

Clues: 210/Answer: 247.

What's the Point?

Why does a woman always use a square pencil in the course of her work?

Clues: 214/Answer: 250.

The Office Job

A man applied for a job in an office. When he arrived at the busy, noisy office he was told by the receptionist to fill out a form and then wait until called. He completed the form and then sat and waited along with four other candidates who had arrived earlier. After a few minutes, he got up and went into an inner office and was subsequently given the job. The other candidates who had arrived earlier were angry. The manager explained why the man had been given the job. What was the reason?

Clues: 209/Answer: 246.

Hearty Appetite

A whale ate normally and many people were very disappointed. Why?

Clues: 206/Answer: 244.

The Upset Bird Watcher

A keen ornithologist saw a rare bird that he had never seen before, except in illustrations. However, he was very upset. Then he was frightened. Why?

Clues: 213/Answer: 250.

Floating Home

A man went on a long trip and was gone several weeks. When he returned, he was found floating at sea. How come?

Clues: 205/Answer: 243.

Co-lateral Damage

During World War II, U.S. forces lost many bombers in raids over Germany due to antiaircraft fire. From the damage on returning bombers, they were able to build up a clear picture of which parts of the planes were hit most frequently and which weren't hit at all. How did they use this information to reduce losses?

Clues: 204/Answer: 241.

Orson Cart

When Orson Welles caused nation-wide panic with his radio broadcast of the Martian landing, there was one group that wasn't fooled. Who were they?

Clues: 209/Answer: 246.

Throwing His Weight About

Why did a man who was not suicidal and not threatened in any way throw himself through a plate-glass window on the 24th floor of an office building and so fall to his death?

Clues: 212/Answer: 249.

Disconnected?

A horse walked all day. Two of its legs traveled 21 miles and two legs traveled 20 miles. How come?

Clues: 204/Answer: 242.

Joker

Four people were playing cards. One played a card and another player immediately jumped up and started to take her clothes off. Why?

Clues: 207/Answer: 244.

Rich Man, Poor Man

In England, why did rich people pour their tea first and then add milk while poor people poured milk first and then added tea?

Clues: 210/Answer: 247.

Mined Over Matter

A sailor at the bow of his ship saw a mine floating in the water directly in the path of the vessel. There was no time to change the ship's direction. How did he avert disaster?

Clues: 208/Answer: 245.

Surprise Visit

A factory manager gets a tip that the company chairman is on his way to pay a surprise visit. The manager orders the staff to clean the factory, clear out all the trash, and hide it away, but the chairman wasn't impressed. Why not?

Clues: 212/Answer: 249.

▼◀ ▲▼◀ ▲▼◀ ▲▼◀ ▲▼◀

The Deadly Stone

A man shot himself because he saw a stone with a small drop of blood on it. Why?

Clues: 204/Answer: 242.

▼◀ ▲▼◀ ▲▼◀ ▲▼◀ ▲▼◀

School's Out

Why does an elderly lady receive a court order to go to school immediately?

Clues: 210/Answer: 247.

The Costly Wave

A man waved his hands in the air and this action cost him $30,000. Why?

Clues: 204/Answer: 241.

WALLY Test 2

Time for another WALLY Test. The questions may look easy, but be warned—they're designed to trip you up. Write down your answers on a piece of paper and then see how many you got right. The time limit is three minutes.

1. What gets higher as it falls?

2. How do you stop moles from digging in your garden?

3. Why did the overweight actor fall through the theater floor?

4. What happened to the man who invented the silent alarm clock?

5. What's the best known star with a tail?

6. How did an actor get his name up in lights in every theater in the country?

7. Where would you find a square ring?

8. What do you give a bald rabbit?

9. How do you make a slow horse fast?

10. Why did Sam wear a pair of pants with three large holes?

Answers on page 273.

2020 Vision

A newspaper editor heard a report that 2020 pigs had been stolen from a farm, so he called the farmer to check the story. The farmer told him the same story, but the editor changed the number for insertion in the news. Why?

Clues: 213/Answer: 249.

THAT'S RIGHT...STOLEN. NO, WAIT, DON'T COME OUT HERE.

The Gap

A man was writing the word HIM. Why did he deliberately leave a gap between the final two letters so that it looked a little like HI M?

Clues: 205-206/Answer: 243.

The Dinner Clue

A suspect is interrogated for several hours but doesn't crack. He then demands a meal and soon afterward the police charge him with murder. Why?

Clues: 204/Answer: 242.

The Deadly Omelet

A man went into a country inn and ordered an omelet for lunch. He was promptly arrested and later executed. Why?

Clues: 204/Answer: 242.

Wrong Way

Why does a man who wants to catch a bus going from Alewife to Zebedee deliberately catch one going the opposite way—from Zebedee to Alewife?

Clues: 214/Answer: 251.

The Single Word

A woman whom I had never met before was introduced to me. I didn't say a word. She told me about herself, but I didn't say a word. She told me many more things about herself, but I didn't say a word. Eventually I said one word and she was very disappointed. What was the word?

Clues: 211/Answer: 248.

Not Eating?

A hungry man has food on his plate but doesn't eat it. Why?

Clues: 209/Answer: 246.

Eensy Weensy Spider Farm

In some parts of France there are spider farms. Why would anybody want to farm spiders?

Clues: 205/Answer: 242.

I'LL HAVE THE SNAILS, THE CALF'S BRAIN AND PANCREAS, AND FOR DESSERT, THE CHOCOLATE BLACK WIDOW CAKE.

Up in Smoke

A man owned some excellent cigars, which he smoked. As a result of this he gained $10,000 and a prison sentence. How?

Clues: 213/Answer: 250.

Two Pigs

A farmer has two pigs that are identical twins from the same litter. However, when he sells them he gets 100 times more for one than the other. Why?

Clues: 213/Answer: 249.

Face-off

In World War I, the French and Austrian armies faced each other. Neither side attacked the other nor fired a shot at the other, yet thousands were killed. How?

Clues: 205/Answer: 243.

Cheap and Cheerful

A man at a party is offered a choice of a certain food—either the expensive fresh variety or the cheaper canned variety. Why does he choose the cheaper canned food?

Clues: 203/Answer: 241.

The Man Who Would Not Read

A tourist in England was traveling by train. He had a book with him that he wanted to read, but he didn't start it until he got off the train. Why?

Clues: 208/Answer: 245.

My Condiments to the Chef

Why did the owner of a café replace all the bottles of condiments on his tables with packets?

Clues: 208/Answer: 246.

Silly Cone

How did an office manager achieve greater efficiency using cones?

Clues: 211/Answer: 248.

Vase and Means

How did the ancient potters discover the ingredient that made perfect china?

Clues: 213/Answer: 250.

The Man Who Did Not Fly

Why was a fictitious name added to an airline's passenger list?

Clues: 208/Answer: 245.

Inheritance

In ancient Ireland, a king had two sons, each of whom wanted to inherit the kingdom. The king decreed that each should be put in a separate rowboat about one mile from shore and told to row in. The first to touch the shore would inherit the kingdom. The elder and stronger son rowed more quickly and was about to touch the shore with the younger son some 20 yards behind him and farther out to sea. How did the younger son inherit the kingdom?

Clues: 206/Answer: 244.

Rock of Ages

A man suffered a serious injury because he was listening to rock-and-roll music. What happened?

Clues: 210/Answer: 247.

▼ ◄ ▲ ▼ ◄ ▲ ▼ ◄ ▲ ▼ ◄ ▲ ▼ ◄

Quo Vadis?

How was an archaeologist in Britain able to deduce that the Romans drove their chariots on the left-hand side of the road?

Clues: 210/Answer: 247.

▼ ◄ ▲ ▼ ◄ ▲ ▼ ◄ ▲ ▼ ◄ ▲ ▼ ◄

Small Is Not Beautiful

Why were small cars banned in Sweden?

Clues: 211/Answer: 248.

Stamp Dearth Death

A man died because he didn't buy enough stamps. What happened?

Clues: 212/Answer: 248-249.

The Last Mail

A man mailed two letters to the same address at the same time in the same post office. The letters were identical but the postage on one letter was more than on the other. Why?

Clues: 207/Answer: 245.

Pork Puzzler

Why did a man who didn't like bacon always pack some bacon when he went on a trip, and throw it out when he arrived?

Clues: 209/Answer: 246.

The Deadly Feather

A man lies dead next to a feather that caused his death. What happened?

Clues: 204/Answer: 242.

Frozen Assets

Why did they build a railway line over the ice when the place could be reached by land and they knew the ice would melt anyway?

Clues: 205/Answer: 243.

Turned Off

A man inadvertently caused all radio station transmissions in the world to cease. How? And who was he?

Clues: 213/Answer: 249.

Publicity Puzzler

A man put an ad in the newspaper. As a result of this, he and another man go shopping together twice a year, but have no other contact. Why?

Clues: 209-210/Answer: 247.

Who Wants It Anyway?

He who has it is worried. He who loses it is poorer. He who wins it no longer has it. What is it?

Clue: 214/Answer: 251.

The Sealed Room

A perfectly healthy man was trapped in a sealed room. He died, but not from lack of oxygen. What did he die of?

Clues: 210/Answer: 248.

Knights of Old

What action carried out by knights because of their armor has persisted to this day, when no one wears armor?

Clues: 207/Answer: 244.

Shave That Pig!

"Barber, Barber, shave a pig" goes an old nursery rhyme. Why would anyone want to shave a live pig?

Clues: 211/Answer: 248.

Murder Mystery

A woman murders her husband. She gains no advantage for herself in doing so. The police knew she did it. She was never charged with murder. What was going on?

Clues: 208/Answer: 246.

Written Down

A woman is writing in capital letters. She has difficulty writing the letters A, E, F, G, H, and L, but no difficulty with C, K, M, N, V, and W. Why?

Clues: 214/Answer: 251.

Watch Out!

A man left his house to get a drink but died because his watch stopped. Why?

Clues: 213/Answer: 250.

The Wedding Present

A man bought a beautiful and appropriate wedding gift for a friend's wedding. The gift was wrapped and sent. When the gift was opened at the wedding, the man was highly embarrassed. Why?

Clues: 214/Answer: 250.

Not the Führer

A body that looked very like that of Adolf Hitler was found by advancing Allied troops near Hitler's bunker in Berlin. The face was destroyed. How did the soldiers quickly find out that it wasn't Hitler's body?

Clues: 209/Answer: 246.

Angry Response

A man called his wife from the office to say that he would be home at around eight o'clock. He got in at two minutes past eight. His wife was extremely angry at his late arrival. Why?

Clues: 215/Answer: 252.

Alone in a Boat

Why are two little animals alone in a little boat in the middle of the ocean?

Clues: 215/Answer: 251.

Picture Purchase

An art expert went to a sale and bought a picture he knew to be worthless. Why?

Clues: 221/Answer: 258.

Golf Bag

During a golf competition, Paul's ball ended up in a bunker inside a little brown paper bag that had blown onto the course. He was told that he must either play the ball in the bag or take the ball out of the bag and incur a one stroke penalty. What did he do?

Clues: 219/Answer: 255.

Complete Garbage

The garbage was emptied out of the cans and a man died. How?

Clues: 217/Answer: 253.

Strangulation

A famous dancer was found strangled. The police did not suspect murder. Why not?

Clues: 224/Answer: 260.

Flipping Pages

Yesterday, I went through a book, which I had already read, in a peculiar manner. After I finished a page, I flipped to the next page, then rotated the book 180 degrees. After that page, I rotated the book 180 degrees and then flipped to the next page, rotated the book 180 degrees again, and continued in this fashion until I was done with the whole book. What was going on?

Clues: 218/Answer: 254.

▼◄ ▲ ▼◄ ▲ ▼◄ ▲ ▼◄ ▲ ▼◄

Leadfoot and Gumshoe

A woman is stopped for speeding. The police officer gives her a warning, but the woman insists that she be given a ticket and a fine, which she promptly pays. Why did she want the ticket and fine?

Clues: 219/Answer: 256.

▼◄ ▲ ▼◄ ▲ ▼◄ ▲ ▼◄ ▲ ▼◄

Russian Racer

At the height of the Cold War, a U.S. racing car easily beat a Russian car in a two-car race. How did the Russian newspapers truthfully report this in order to make it look as though the Russian car had outdone the American car?

Clues: 222/Answer: 259.

Straight Ahead

When the Eisenhower Interstate Highway System was built, it was specified that one mile in every five must be absolutely straight. Why?

Clues: 224/Answer: 260.

Motion Not Passed

A referendum motion was not passed. If more people had voted against it, however, it would have passed. How come?

Clues: 220/Answer: 256.

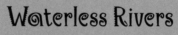

Waterless Rivers

Now for a riddle: What has rivers but no water, cities but no buildings, and forests but no trees?

Clues: 225/Answer: 261.

Man in Tights

A man wearing tights is lying unconscious in a field. Next to him is a rock. What happened?

Clues: 219/Answer: 256.

The Test

The teacher gave Ben and Jerry a written test. Ben read the test, then folded his arms and answered none of the questions. Jerry carefully wrote out good answers to the questions. When the time was up, Ben handed in a blank sheet of paper while Jerry handed in his work. The teacher gave Ben an A and Jerry a C. Why?

Clues: 224/Answer: 260.

Fired for Joining Mensa

Mensa is a club for clever people. Anne's employer has no anti-Mensa feeling, but has made it clear to her that if she ever joins Mensa she will lose her job. How come?

Clues: 218/Answer: 254.

Statue of an Insect

Why is there a commemorative statue of an insect in a little town in the state of Alabama?

Clues: 224/Answer: 260.

Six-Foot Drop

A man standing on solid concrete dropped a tomato six feet, but it did not break or bruise. How come?

Clues: 223/Answer: 259.

Seven Bells

A little shop in New York is called The Seven Bells, yet it has eight bells hanging outside. Why?

Clues: 223/Answer: 259.

〜〜〜〜〜〜〜〜〜〜〜〜〜〜

Reentry

What took 19 years to get into itself?

Clues: 222/Answer: 258.

Assault and Battery

John is guilty of no crime, but he is surrounded by professional people, one of whom hits him until he cries. Why?

Clues: 215/Answer: 252.

Up i̶

One hundred feet
its back on the gro

Clean-Shaven

Why did Alexander the Great order all his men to shave?

Clues: 216/Answer: 253.

Adolf Hitler

During the war, a British soldier had Adolf Hitler clearly in the sights of his gun. Why didn't he fire?

Clues: 214/Answer: 251.

...ning Numbers

...ve on a piece of paper the winning ...umbers in next week's lotto jackpot. I am an avid gambler, yet I feel I have very little chance of winning. Why?

Clues: 226/Answer: 261.

Riddle of the Sphinx

The Sphinx asked this famous riddle: What is it that goes on four legs in the morning, two legs in the afternoon, and three legs in the evening?

Clues: 222/Answer: 258.

▼ ◄ ▲ ▼ ◄ ▲ ▼ ◄ ▲ ▼ ◄ ▲ ▼ ◄

Fair Fight

A boxer left the ring after winning the world championship. His trainer took all the money and he never got a cent. Why not?

Clues: 217/Answer: 254.

Unclimbed

Why has no one climbed the largest known extinct volcano?

Clues: 225/Answer: 261.

▼ ◄ ▲ ▼ ◄ ▲ ▼ ◄ ▲ ▼ ◄ ▲ ▼ ◄

Talking to Herself

A woman is talking sadly. Nobody can understand her, but a man is filming her intently. Why?

Clues: 224/Answer: 260.

Unknown Recognition

I saw a man I had never seen before, but I immediately knew who he was. He was not famous and had never been described to me. He was not unusual nor doing anything unusual. How did I recognize him?

Clues: 225/Answer: 261.

The Unlucky Bed

A certain bed in a certain hospital acquires the reputation of being unlucky. Whatever patient is assigned to this bed seems to die there on a Friday evening. A watch is kept by camera and the reason is discovered. What is it?

Clues: 225/Answer: 261.

Once Too Often

If you do it once, it's good. If you do it twice on the same day, though, it's a serious crime. What is it?

Clues: 221/Answer: 257.

Missing Items

What two items does a boy have at 10 years of age that he did not have when he was 1 year old?

Clues: 220/Answer: 256.

Noteworthy

A woman took a picture of a U.S. president to her bank. As a result a criminal was arrested. How?

Clues: 220/Answer: 257.

Rejected Shoes

A man bought a pair of shoes that were in good condition and that fit him well. He liked the style and they looked good. However, after he had worn them for one day he took them back to the shop and asked for a refund. Why?

Clues: 222/Answer: 258.

Slow Drive

Why does a man drive his car on a long journey at a steady 15 miles per hour? The speed limit is well above that and his car is in full working order and capable of high speeds.

Clues: 223/Answer: 259.

Weak Case

The police charged a man with a crime. They had a weak case against him. He posted his bail. The police then had a strong case against him. Why?

Clues: 225/Answer:261.

The Writer

A man who was paralyzed in his arms, legs, and mouth, and unable to speak a word, wrote a best-selling book. How?

Clues: 226/Answer: 262.

The Man Who Got Water

A man parked his car on the road, walked into a building, returned with some water, and poured the water onto the sidewalk. Why?

Clues: 220/Answer: 256.

Chimney Problem

An industrial archaeologist was examining an abandoned factory in a remote place with no one in sight or within earshot. He climbed to the top of an old 100-foot chimney by means of a rusty old ladder attached to the outside of the chimney. When he got to the top, the ladder fell away, leaving him stranded. How did he get down?

Clues: 216/Answer: 253.

Happy Birthday

A man went into his local shopping center. A woman whom he had never met before wished him a happy birthday. How did she know it was his birthday?

Clues: 219/Answer: 255.

Acidic Action

A murderer killed his wife and dissolved her body completely in a bath of acid. What piece of evidence caused him to be caught?

Clues: 214/Answer: 251.

November 11

A large mail order company performed an analysis of its customers. It was surprised to learn that an unusually large number were born on November 11. How could this be?

Clues: 221/Answer: 257.

Garbage Nosiness

One morning last week I peered into my neighbor's garbage can and then drove to work feeling annoyed. One morning this week I peered into my other neighbor's garbage can and then drove off feeling even more annoyed. Why?

Clues: 218/Answer: 255.

Bottled Up

A cleaning woman asked the man she worked for if she could take home his empty bottles. When she got home, she threw them out. Why did she do this?

Clues: 216/Answer: 252.

Well-Meaning

How did an animal rights activist who had good intentions cause the death of the living creatures she was trying to save?

Clues: 225/Answer: 261.

Shooting a Dead Man

A policeman shot a dead man. He was not acting illegally. Why did he do it?

Clues: 223/Answer: 259.

Alex Ferguson

In the early 1990s, Alex Ferguson was the coach of Manchester United, the most successful professional soccer team in England at that time. Previously he had been a very successful manager in Scotland. He would be a very successful manager of a soccer team anywhere in the world, except Singapore. Why is that?

Clues: 215/Answer: 251.

Don't Get Up

A woman is reading a newspaper alone. She hears the phone ring in the room next to the one she is in. Although she knows that the call is probably important, she does not bother to answer it. Why not?

Clues: 217/Answer: 254.

Misunderstood

Part of the police manual gives instructions in a language that none of the policemen speaks. Why?

Clues: 220/Answer: 256.

Scuba Do

Why was a man driving down the street wearing a scuba face mask?

Clues: 223/Answer: 259.

WALLY Test 3

From the World Association of Learning, Laughter, and Youth (WALLY) comes the WALLY Test! It is a set of quick-fire questions. They may look easy, but be warned—they are designed to trick you. Write down your answers on a piece of paper and then see how many you got right. The time limit is three minutes.

1. What is the last thing you take off before going to bed at night?

2. What gets longer when it is cut at both ends?

3. What was the first name of King George VI of England?

4. What do you call a fly without wings?

5. How many squares are there on a standard chessboard?

6. How many seconds are there in a year?

7. A man throws a ball three feet, it stops, and then returns to his hand without touching anything. How come?

8. What was the largest island in the world before Australia was discovered?

9. Why can a policeman never open the door in his pajamas?

10. If 5 dogs kill 5 rats in 5 minutes, how long does it take 15 dogs to kill 15 rats?

Answers on page 273-274.

One Mile

If you go to your atlas and look at the western edge of the state of South Dakota where it borders Montana, you will see a straight line with a kink of about one mile. Everywhere else the border is a straight line. The kink does not benefit any local landowner and no other states are involved. Why is the kink there?

Clues: 221/Answer: 257.

The Unbroken Arm

Why did a perfectly healthy young girl put a full plaster cast on her arm when it was not injured in any way?

Clues: 224/Answer: 260.

Exceptional Gratitude

Why did Bill thank Ted for some eggs that Bill had never received and that Ted had never given?

Clues: 217/Answer: 254.

The Shoplifter

A shoplifter starts stealing small items and over a period of time steals larger and larger items, but then suddenly stops altogether. What is going on?

Clues: 223/Answer: 259.

88 Too Big

A man died because his number was 88 too big. How come?

Clues: 217/Answer: 254.

Getting Away with Murder

A man shot his wife dead. She was not threatening him or anyone else. He then gave himself up to the police. They released him. Why?

Clues: 218-219/Answer: 255.

The Power of Tourism

In a certain place the local authorities, in order to increase tourism, have made the price of electricity higher. Why?

Clues: 221-222/Answer: 258.

Dali's Brother

Some time after Salvador Dali's death, his younger brother became famous as (believe it or not) a surrealist painter. This younger brother had great international success and the word "genius" was used to describe him. His name was Dali and he did not change it. Yet today, the world remembers only one Dali and few people even know that he had a brother. Why is this?

Clues: 217/Answer: 253.

Wiped Out

A woman got a job with a large company. After her first day's work she returned home utterly exhausted because of a misunderstanding. What had happened?

Clues: 226/Answer: 261.

Bare Bone

During an examination, a me is handed a human femur (thigh bone). The examiner asks the student, "How many of these do you have?"
The student replies, "Five."
"Wrong," says the examiner, "You have two femurs."
But the student was right. How come?

Clues: 215/Answer: 252.

Poor Investment

Why did a company spend millions of dollars trying to find something that costs only a few thousand dollars?

Clues: 221/Answer: 258.

Two Clocks

A man was given two clocks by his wife as a Christmas present. He did not collect clocks and they already had plenty of clocks in the house. However, he was very pleased to receive them. Why?

Clues: 224/Answer: 260.

Nonexistent Actors

Why did the credits of a well-known movie list the names of four nonexistent actors?

Clues: 220/Answer: 257.

Machine Forge

A man builds a machine into which he feeds colored paper. Out of the other side come perfect $100 bills. Experts cannot tell them from real ones. How does he do it and why does he sell the machine?

Clues: 219/Answer: 256.

▼ ◀ ▲ ▼ ◀ ▲ ▼ ◀ ▲ ▼ ◀ ▲ ▼ ◀

Invisible

What can you stand in front of in broad daylight and not see, even if you have perfect eyesight?

Clues: 219/Answer: 256.

▼ ◀ ▲ ▼ ◀ ▲ ▼ ◀ ▲ ▼ ◀ ▲ ▼ ◀

Job Description

Two men were sitting in a crowded restaurant. A woman who was a total stranger to both of them walked in and told them her job. She said nothing more and they said nothing. What was going on?

Clues: 219/Answer: 256.

The Auction

A man went to an auction to bid for something he wanted. He expected to pay about $100 for it, but ended up paying $500. There was no minimum price and no one bid against him. What happened?

Clues: 215/Answer: 252.

Promotion

John is a young man working for a big company. He is lazy, poorly motivated, and inefficient. Yet he is the first person in his department to be promoted. Why?

Clues: 222/Answer: 258.

Wonder Horse

A horse that had lost every one of its previous races was entered in a horse race and came in first ahead of a top-class field. No drugs were used, and if the jockey had not confessed, then nobody would have known. What happened?

Clues: 226/Answer: 262.

Spraying the Grass

The groundskeeper at a sports complex watered the grass every evening when the sun was setting. The grass grew fine. Before a major event, though, he sprayed the grass during the midday heat. Why?

Clues: 224/Answer: 260.

Barren Patch

A farmer has a patch of ground in the middle of one of his most fertile fields on which nothing will grow. Why not?

Clues: 215-216/Answer: 252.

Shaking a Fist

A policeman stopped a man for dangerous driving. As the policeman walked toward the car, the man rolled down the window and waved his fist at the policeman. Later, he thanked the policeman for saving his life. Why?

Clues: 223/Answer: 259.

Adrift in the Ocean

Two men are in a boat drifting in the Atlantic Ocean a hundred miles from the nearest land. They have no drinking water onboard, no radio, and they have no contact with any other boats or people. Yet they survive for a long time. How?

Clues: 215/Answer: 251.

No More Bore

A notorious bore once called on Winston Churchill, who sent his butler to the door to say that Churchill was not at home. What suggestion did Churchill make to the butler to convince the caller that he really was not at home?

Clues: 220/Answer: 256.

Gas Attack

A man was sentenced to ten years' imprisonment with hard labor because he had kept the gas mask that the army had issued him. Why?

Clues: 218/Answer: 255.

Burnt Wood

Over the past 100 years many men have dedicated significant portions of their lives to the quest for some burnt wood. Although they have sometimes been successful, the burnt wood has never moved. What is it?

Clues: 216/Answer: 252.

Window Pain

A builder builds a house that has a square window. It is two feet high and two feet wide. It is not covered by anything. The person for whom the house is being built decides that the window does not give enough light. He tells the builder to change the window so that it gives twice the amount of light. It must be in the same wall, and it must be a square window that is two feet high and two feet wide. How does the builder accomplish this task?

Clues: 225/Answer: 261.

The Wrong Ball

A golfer drove his ball out of sight over a hill. When he got there, he saw a ball that was the same make as his own and identical to it in every way. But he knew immediately that it was not his ball. How come?

Clues: 226/Answer: 262.

HEY, DUANE? IS THAT YOU?

NICK? WE THOUGHT YOU'D DROWNED.

WALLY Test 4

Time for another WALLY Test. The questions may look easy, but be warned—they're designed to trip you up. Write down your answers on a piece of paper and then see how many you got right. The time limit is three minutes.

1. Rearrange these letters to make one new word: NEW NEW DOOR

2. What do you find in seconds, minutes, and centuries, but not in days, years, or decades?

3. Which is correct: "Seven eights are 54" or "Seven eights is 54"?

4. Three men in a boat each had a cigarette, but they had no match, fire, or lighter. How did they light the cigarettes?

5. A clock strikes 6 in five seconds. How long does it take to strike 12?

6. What was the U.S. president's name in 1984?

7. Who won an Oscar for Best Actor and an Olympic gold medal for sprinting?

8. If two men can dig two holes in two days, how long does it take one man to dig half a hole?

9. An 80-year-old prisoner was kept inside a high security prison with all the doors locked. He broke out. How?

10. If the post office clerk refused to stick a $4 stamp on your package, would you stick it on yourself?

Answers on page 274.

Bald Facts

A woman fell in love and, as a result, lost all her hair. Why?

Clues: 215/Answer: 252.

Fingerprint Evidence

The mass murderer Ted Bundy was very careful never to leave any fingerprints at the scene of any of his crimes, and he never did. Yet fingerprint evidence helped to incriminate him. How come?

Clues: 218/Answer: 254.

▼ ◄ ▲ ▼ ◄ ▲ ▼ ◄ ▲ ▼ ◄ ▲ ▼ ◄

Pentagon Puzzle

The headquarters of the U.S. defense operations is the Pentagon in Arlington, Virginia. Why does it have twice as many bathrooms as it needs?

Clues: 221/Answer: 257.

▼ ◄ ▲ ▼ ◄ ▲ ▼ ◄ ▲ ▼ ◄ ▲ ▼ ◄

Hosing Down

Because it was raining, the firemen hosed down the road. Why?

Clues: 219/Answer: 255.

~~~~~~~~~~~~~~~~~~~~~~~~~~~~~

You Can't Be Too Careful

Millions of people buy a particular medicine. The disease for which the medicine is effective is one that these people have virtually no chance of catching. What do they buy?

Clues: 226/Answer: 262.

Three Spirals

A woman was pleased when she received three spirals instead of the usual two. When it was discovered that she had received three spirals, she was arrested. Why?

Clues: 224/Answer: 260.

Fill Her Up!

A woman bought her husband a beautiful new sports car as a present. When he first saw it, he filled it with wet cement and completely ruined it. Why?

Clues: 218/Answer: 254.

Nonconventional

In a convent, the novice nuns at the dinner table are not allowed to ask for anything such as the salt from the other end of the table. This is because they should be so aware of one another's needs that they should not need to ask. How do they get around this prohibition?

Clues: 220/Answer: 257.

Replacing the Leaves

During fall, a little girl was in her backyard trying to stick the fallen leaves back onto the trees with glue. Why?

Clues: 222/Answer: 258.

Secret Assignment

The famous physicist Ulam one day noticed that several of his best graduate students had disappeared from his university. They had in fact gone to Los Alamos to take part in the top-secret preparations for the first atomic bomb. They were sworn to secrecy. How did Ulam find out where they had gone?

Clues: 223/Answer: 259.

Debugging

How were insects once used in the diagnosis of a serious disease?

Clues: 217/Answer: 253.

The Ransom Note

A kidnapper sent a ransom note. He prepared it carefully and ensured that it contained no fingerprints. Yet it was used to prove his guilt. How?

Clues: 222/Answer: 258.

Biography

An author died because he wrote a biography. How did he die?

Clues: 216/Answer: 252.

The Carpet Seller

I bought a beautiful plain carpet measuring 9 feet by 16 feet from the carpet seller. When I got home I realized that my room was actually 12 feet by 12 feet. I returned to the carpet seller, who assured me that I could now exactly fit my room, provided I made just one cut to the original piece. Can you figure out how to do it?

Clues: 216/Answer: 253.

Ancient Antics

We generally consider ourselves to be a lot smarter and better educated than the people who lived in the prehistoric periods of the Stone Age, Iron Age, and Bronze Age. But what was it that men and women did in those times that no man or woman has managed to achieve for the last 4000 years?

Clues: 215/Answer: 251.

Walking Backward

A man walked backward from the front door of his house to his kitchen. Someone rang the doorbell and the man ran quickly out of his back door. Why?

Clues: 225/Answer: 261.

Cartoon Character

What cartoon character owes his existence to a misprint in a scientific journal?

Clues: 216/Answer: 253.

Full Refund

A young couple went to a theater to watch a movie. After 15 minutes they decided to leave. They had had a perfectly good view of the movie, which was running in perfect order. The cashier gave them a full refund. Why?

Clues: 218/Answer: 254-255.

Free Lunch

A man in a restaurant used two forks and one knife. He did not pay for his lunch. What was happening?

Clues: 218/Answer: 254.

No Response

A man often answered questions in the course of his work. One day a stranger asked him a perfectly reasonable question that he refused to answer. Why?

Clues: 220/Answer: 257.

Right Off

A man comes out of his house to find that his new car is damaged beyond repair after he has paid for it but before he has had time to insure it. However, he is absolutely delighted at what has happened. Why?

Clues: 222/Answer: 258.

A Day at the Races

A man was returning from a day at the races where he had made a lot of money. He was speeding in his car and was stopped by the police. The policeman took down all his details, but the man was never prosecuted or suffered any penalty. Why not?

Clues: 217/Answer: 253.

Business Rivalry

Cain and Abel are business rivals. Cain cuts his price, and Abel then undercuts him. Cain then cuts his price even lower than Abel. Abel slashes his price to a ridiculous level and gets all the business, forcing Cain out of the market. But Cain has the last laugh. Why?

Clues: 216/Answer: 253.

Pass Protection

In the city where I live, commuters on the mass transit system can use monthly passes or single tokens. Today, I saw long lines of commuters waiting to buy passes and tokens. Those people with passes or tokens were able to bypass the lines. However, even though I had neither a pass nor a token, I was also able to walk right up to the turnstiles and pass through. How come?

Clues: 221/Answer: 257.

The Deadly Sculpture

A penniless sculptor made a beautiful metal statue, which he sold. Because of this he died soon afterward. Why?

Clues: 228/Answer: 263.

THANKS FOR HELPING ME TIE DOWN THE STATUE I JUST SOLD. I PROMISE I'LL MEET YOU AT THE DIVORCE LAWYER'S AS SOON AS I DELIVER IT.

Adam Had None

Adam had none. Eve had two. Everyone nowadays has three. What are they?

Clues: 226/Answer: 262.

The Fatal Fish

A man was preparing a fish to eat for a meal when he made a mistake. He then knew that he would shortly die. How?

Clues: 229-230/Answer: 264.

Peak Performance

The body of a climber is found many years after his death a thousand feet below the summit of one of the world's highest mountains. In his pocket is a diary claiming that he had reached the summit and was on his way down. How was it discovered that he was not telling the truth?

Clues: 233/Answer: 267.

Shot Dead

A woman who was in a house saw a stranger walking down the road. She took a gun and shot him dead. The next day she did the same thing to another stranger. Other people saw her do it and knew that she had killed the two men, yet she was never arrested or charged. Why not?

Clues: 235/Answer: 269.

Would You Believe It?

Three people were holding identical blocks of wood. They released the blocks at the same time. The blocks of wood were not attached to anything. The first person's block fell downward. The second person's block rose up. The third person's block stayed where it was, unsupported. What was going on?

Clues: 238/Answer: 271.

▼◀ ▲ ▼◀ ▲ ▼◀ ▲ ▼◀ ▲ ▼◀

Sitting Ducks

Why does a woman with no interest in hunting buy a gun for shooting ducks?

Clues: 236/Answer: 269.

▼◀ ▲ ▼◀ ▲ ▼◀ ▲ ▼◀ ▲ ▼◀

Jailbreak

A man planned his escape from prison very carefully. He could have carried it out in the dead of night but he preferred to do it in the middle of the morning. Why?

Clues: 231/Answer: 266.

66

Bald Facts

Mary, Queen of Scots was almost totally bald, and wore a wig to conceal this fact from her subjects. How was her secret revealed?

Clues: 227/Answer: 263.

Lethal Action

Brazilian authorities took actions to protect their fruit crops, and ten people from another continent died. How?

Clues: 231/Answer: 266.

YOU TWO SMUGGLING ANY FRUITS TODAY?

CUSTOMS

Recognition

John lived in England all his life, until his parents died. He then went to Australia to visit relatives. His Aunt Mary had left England before he was born and had never returned. He had never met his Aunt Mary, had never spoken to her, and had never seen a picture of her. Yet he recognized her immediately in a crowded airport. How?

Clues: 234-235/Answer: 268.

Destruction

Commercial premises are destroyed by a customer. Afterward he disappears, but even if he had been caught he could not have been charged. Why?

Clues: 228-229/Answer: 264.

Pesky Escalator

A foreign visitor to London wanted to ride up the escalator at the subway station, but did not do so. Why?

Clues: 233/Answer: 268.

Wonderful Walk

A man and his dog went for a walk in the woods. When he returned home he invented something now worth millions of dollars. What was it?

Clues: 238/Answer: 271.

Poles Apart

How did early explorers economize with provisions for a polar expedition?

Clues: 233/Answer: 268.

Arrested Development

A bank robber grabbed several thousand dollars from a bank counter and, although he was armed, he was captured within a few seconds before he could leave the bank. How?

Clues: 226/Answer: 262.

Holed Out

A golfer dreamed all his life of getting a hole in one. However, when he eventually did get a hole in one, he was very unhappy and, in fact, quit golf altogether. Why?

Clues: 231/Answer: 265.

Trunk-ated

The police stop a car and they suspect that the trunk contains evidence linking the driver with a serious crime. However, they do not have a search warrant and if they open the trunk forcibly without probable cause, any evidence uncovered will not be admissible in court. How do they proceed?

Clues: 237/Answer: 270.

Sports Mad

Why was a keen sports fan rushing around his house looking for a roll of sticky tape?

Clues: 236/Answer: 269.

Appendectomy I & II

(There are two different solutions to this puzzle. Try both before looking at the answer to either.)

Why did a surgeon remove a perfectly healthy appendix?

Clues: 226/Answers: 262.

WOW, YOU DO HAVE GOOD MEDICAL COVERAGE. AN APPENDIX TRANSPLANT UNDER THE HYPOCHONDRIAC CLAUSE.

Riotous Assembly

After riots in a large institution, one section did not reopen for a long time after the other sections. Why?

Clues: 235/Answer: 268.

Kneed to Know

A woman places her hand on her husband's knee for an hour and then takes it off for ten minutes; then she places her hand on her husband's knee for another hour. Why?

Clues: 231/Answer: 266.

Bad Trip

An anti-drug agency distributed material to children in school. However, this had the opposite effect to what was intended. Why?

Clues: 227/Answer: 262.

WALLY Test 5

From the World Association of Learning, Laughter, and Youth (WALLY) comes the WALLY Test! It is a set of quick-fire questions. They may look easy, but be warned—they are designed to trick you. Write down your answers on a piece of paper and then see how many you got right. The time limit is three minutes.

1. When you see geese flying in a V formation, why is it that one leg of the V is always longer than the other?

2. Why are there so many Smiths in the telephone directory?

3. What is E.T. short for?

4. Where do you find a no-legged dog?

5. Approximately how many house bricks does it take to complete a brick house in England?

6. How do you stop a bull from charging?

7. What cheese is made backward?

8. Take away my first letter; I remain the same. Now take away my fourth letter; I remain the same. Now take away my last letter; I remain the same. What am I?

9. If a white man threw a black stone into the Red Sea, what would it become?

10. How do you make a bandstand?

Answers on page 274.

Two Letters

Why did a man write the same two letters over and over again on a piece of paper?

Clues: 237/Answer: 270.

Shakespeare's Blunder

What major scientific blunder did Shakespeare include in his play Twelfth Night?

Clues: 235/Answer: 269.

Body of Evidence

A woman goes into a police station and destroys vital evidence relating to a serious crime, yet she walks away scot-free. How come?

Clues: 227/Answer: 263.

No Charge

A man guilty of a serious crime was arrested. The police had clear evidence against him, but he was set free without charge. Why?

Clues: 232-233/Answer: 267.

Pond Life

Why did the fashion for silk hats in the U.S. lead to a positive environmental increase in the number of small lakes and bogs?

Clues: 234/Answer: 268.

Shoe Shop Shuffle

In a small town there are four shoe shops of about the same size, each carrying more or less the same line in shoes. Yet one shop loses three times as many shoes to theft as each of the other shops. Why?

Clues: 235/Answer: 269.

Caesar's Blunder

Julius Caesar unexpectedly lost many of his ships when he invaded Britain. Why?

Clues: 227/Answer: 263.

Slow Death

The ancient Greek playwright Aeschylus was killed by a tortoise. How?

Clues: 236/Answer: 269.

Driving Away

A man steals a very expensive car owned by a very rich woman. Although he was a very good driver, within a few minutes he was involved in a serious accident. Why?

Clues: 229/Answer: 264.

The Happy Woman

A woman going on a journey used a driver. Then she stopped and used a club to hit a large bird. She was very pleased. Why?

Clues: 230/Answer: 265.

Leonardo's Secret

Leonardo da Vinci created some secret designs for his paintings that he did not want anyone to see. He hid them, but they were recently discovered. How?

Clues: 231/Answer: 266.

Quick on the Draw

Every Saturday night, the national lottery is drawn with a multimillion-dollar first prize. A man sat down in front of his TV on Saturday night and saw that the numbers drawn exactly matched the numbers on his ticket for that day's lottery. He was thrilled but did not win a penny. Why not?

Clues: 234/Answer: 268.

Scaled Down

A butcher tried to deceive a customer by pressing down on the scale while weighing a turkey to make it appear heavier than it was. But the customer's subsequent order forced the butcher to admit his deception. How?

Clues: 235/Answer: 269.

Vandal Scandal

The authorities in Athens were very concerned that tourists sometimes hacked pieces of marble from the columns of the ancient Parthenon buildings. The practice was illegal, but some people seemed determined to take away souvenirs. How did the authorities stop this vandalism?

Clues: 237/Answer: 271.

The Deadly Drawing

A woman walked into a room and saw a new picture there. She immediately knew that someone had been killed. How?

Clues: 228/Answer: 263.

The Letter Left Out

For mathematical reasons, in codes and ciphers it is desirable to have 25 (which is a perfect square) letters rather than the usual 26. Which letter of the English alphabet is left out and why?

Clues: 231/Answer: 266.

Down Periscope

A normal submarine was on the surface of the sea with its hatches open. It sailed due east for two miles. Then it stopped and went down 30 feet. It then sailed another half mile before going down a further 30 feet. All this time it kept its hatches fully open. The crew survived and were not alarmed in any way. What was going on?

Clues: 229/Answer: 264.

REALLY, CAPTAIN, THERE'S
NOTHING TO WORRY ABOUT.

The Mover

What can go from there to here by disappearing and then go from here to there by appearing?

Clues: 232/Answer: 267.

Arrested Development—Again

Two masked men robbed a bank, but they were very quickly picked up by the police. Why?

Clues: 227/Answer: 262.

ALL RIGHT, PAL.
THIS IS A STICKUP.

JOE   ED

Death of a Player

A sportsman was rushed to a hospital from where he was playing and died shortly afterward. Why?

Clues: 228/Answer: 264.

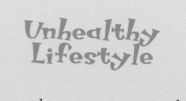

Titanic Proportions

How did the sinking of the Titanic lead directly to the sinking of another ship?

Clues: 236/Answer: 270.

Lit Too Well?

Local government authorities in Sussex, England, installed many more lights than were needed. This resulted in considerable damage, but the authorities were pleased with the results. Why?

Clues: 232/Answer: 266.

Unhealthy Lifestyle

A man and a woman were exploring in the jungle. The woman had a very healthy lifestyle, while the man had a very unhealthy one. At the end of the exploration the woman died suddenly, but the man lived. Why?

Clues: 237/Answer: 270.

Genuine Article

A new play by Shakespeare is discovered. How did the literary experts prove it was authentic?

Clues: 230/Answer: 265.

Hot Picture

A woman paid an artist a large sum to create a picture, and she was very pleased with the results. Yet within a week, under her instructions, the picture was burned. Why?

Clues: 231/Answer: 265.

NO, MA'AM. I DISTINCTLY SAID MY PAINTINGS WERE READY TO BE "FRAMED" NOT "FLAMED."

New World Record

A 102-year-old woman was infirm and inactive, yet one day she was congratulated on setting a new world record. What was it?

Clues: 232/Answer: 267.

Death by Romance

A newly married couple had a fireside supper together. They were so cozy and comfortable that they dozed off on the floor. Next morning they were both found dead where they lay. What had happened?

Clues: 228/Answer: 264.

▽ ◁ ▲ ▽ ◁ ▲ ▽ ◁ ▲ ▽ ◁ ▲ ▽ ▽

Penalty

After a World Cup soccer match, two players swapped jerseys. The police immediately arrested them. Why?

Clues: 233/Answer: 267.

▽ ◁ ▲ ▽ ◁ ▲ ▽ ◁ ▲ ▽ ◁ ▲ ▽ ◁

Golf Challenge I, II & III

(There are three different solutions to this puzzle. Try all three before looking at any of the answers.)

A man and a woman, who were both poor golfers, challenged each other to a match. The man scored 96 while the woman scored 98. However, the woman was declared the winner. Why?

Clues: 230/Answers: 265.

Poor Investment

A man bought a house for $1,000,000 as an investment. The house was well kept and carefully maintained by a good caretaker. Although the house remained in perfect structural order, within a few years it was worthless. Why?

Clues: 234/Answer: 268.

Give Us a Hand ...

A man searching for precious stones didn't find any, but found a severed human hand instead. What had happened?

Clues: 230/Answer: 265.

Evil Intent

A rich man meets a lady at the theater and invites her back to his house for a drink. She has a drink and then leaves. About an hour later he suddenly realizes that she intends to return and burgle his house. How does he know?

Clues: 229/Answer: 264.

Judge for Yourself

The defendant in a major lawsuit asked his lawyer if he should send the judge a box of fine cigars in the hope of influencing him. The lawyer said it was a very bad idea and would prejudice the judge against him. The defendant listened carefully, sent the cigars, and won the case. What happened?

Clues: 231/Answer: 266.

Two Heads Are Better Than One!

Several Americans reported they saw a creature that had two heads, two arms, and four legs. They were surprised, frightened, and alarmed, and when they told their friends, nobody believed them. But they were reliable witnesses. What had they seen?

Clues: 237/Answer: 270.

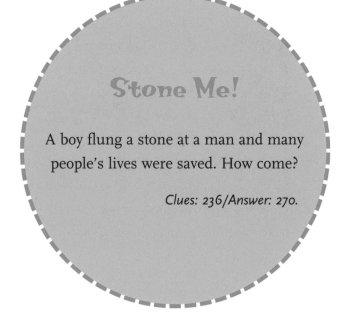

Stone Me!

A boy flung a stone at a man and many people's lives were saved. How come?

Clues: 236/Answer: 270.

Love Letters

Why did a woman send out 1,000 anonymous Valentine's cards to different men?

Clues: 232/Answer: 266.

Tree Trouble

The authorities were concerned that a famous old tree was being damaged because so many tourists came up to it and touched it. So a wall was built around the tree to protect it. But this had the opposite effect of that intended. Why?

Clues: 237/Answer: 270.

Strange Behavior

A man was driving down the road into town with his family on a clear day. He saw a tree and immediately stopped the car and then reversed at high speed. Why?

Clues: 236/Answer: 270.

The Burial Chamber

Why did a man build a beautiful burial chamber, complete with sculptures and paintings, and then deliberately wreck it?

Clues: 227/Answer: 263.

Miscarriage of Justice

An Italian judge released a guilty man and convicted an innocent man and as a result the confectionery industry has greatly benefited. Why?

Clues: 232/Answer: 267.

Offenses Down

The police in Sussex, England, found a new way to complete their form-filling and paperwork that significantly reduced crime. What was it?

Clues: 233/Answer: 267.

Police Chase

A high-speed police car chases a much slower vehicle in which criminals are escaping. But the police fail to catch them. Why?

Clues: 233-234/Answer: 268.

Café Society

A mall café is pestered by teenagers who come in, buy a single cup of coffee, and stay for hours, and thus cut down on available space for other customers. How does the owner get rid of them, quite legally?

Clues: 228/Answer: 263.

Hi, Jean!

A shop owner introduced expensive new procedures to make his premises more hygienic, but the results were the very opposite. Why?

Clues: 230/Answer: 265.

SO, YOU'RE THE NEW PEST CONTROL GUY.

The Empty Machine

A gumball machine dispensed gum when quarters were inserted. When the machine was opened, there was no money inside. A considerable number of gumballs had been consumed and the machine did not appear to have been interfered with in any way. What had happened?

Clues: 229/Answer: 264.

▽◄▲▽◄▲▽◄▲▽◄▲▽◄

Take a Fence

A man painted his garden fence green and then went on holiday. When he came back two weeks later, he was amazed to see that the fence was blue. Nobody had touched the fence. What had happened?

Clues: 236/Answer: 270.

▽◄▲▽◄▲▽◄▲▽◄▲▽◄

WALLY Test 6

Time for another WALLY Test. The questions may look easy, but be warned—they're designed to trip you up. Write down your answers on a piece of paper and then see how many you got right. The time limit is three minutes.

1. What should you give an injured lemon?

2. If an atheist died in church, what would they put on his coffin?

3. Who went into the lion's den unarmed and came out alive?

4. A man rode down the street on a horse, yet walked. How come?

5. How can you eat an egg without breaking the shell?

6. Why was King Henry VIII buried in Westminster Abbey?

7. In China they hang many criminals, but they will not hang a man with a wooden leg. Why?

8. Why do storks stand on one leg?

9. A circular field is covered in thick snow. A black cow with white spots is in the middle. Two white cows with black spots are on the edge of the field. What time is it?

10. What was the problem with the wooden car with wooden wheels and a wooden engine?

Answers on page 274.

Sex Discrimination

When lawyers went to prison to visit their clients they found that female lawyers were searched on entry but male lawyers were not. Why?

Clues: 235/Answer: 269.

THEY SEARCHED YOU WITH A METAL DETECTOR?

YES, AND THEN AFTER THE MEETING AT JUNIOR'S SCHOOL, I WENT TO SEE A CLIENT IN PRISON.

The Parson's Pup

Why did the vicar want only a black dog?

Clues: 233/Answer: 267.

Weight Loss

How did a Japanese diet clinic achieve great weight-loss results for its patients even though they did not change their diet or undertake more activity than normal?

Clues: 237-238/Answer: 271.

Psychic

You enter a parking lot and see a woman walking toward you. You then see a row of cars and know immediately which one is hers. How?

Clues: 234/Answer: 268.

The Happy Robber

A robber holds up a bank, but leaves with no money whatsoever. However, he is more pleased than if he had left with lots of money. Why?

Clues: 230/Answer: 265.

The Cathedral Untouched

When London was bombed during World War II, St. Paul's Cathedral, in the center of the city, was never hit. Why not?

Clues: 228/Answer: 263.

Carrier Bags

During World War II, the British Royal Navy had very few aircraft carriers. What ingenious plan was devised to remedy this deficiency?

Clues: 228/Answer: 263.

Siege Mentality

A city is under siege. The attackers have run out of ammunition and have suffered heavy casualties. Yet they take the city within a few days without further losses. How?

Clues: 235/Answer: 269.

Poor Show

Every time he performed in public, it was a complete flop. Yet he became famous for it, and won medals and prizes. People came from all over and paid to see him perform. Who was he?

Clues: 234/Answer: 268.

▼ ◄ ▲ ▼ ◄ ▲ ▼ ◄ ▲ ▼ ◄ ▲ ▼ ◄

Message Received

How did Alexander the Great send secret messages with his envoy?

Clues: 232/Answer: 266.

▼ ◄ ▲ ▼ ◄ ▲ ▼ ◄ ▲ ▼ ◄ ▲ ▼ ◄

The World's Most Expensive Car

The most expensive car ever made is for sale. Although many people want to own it and can afford to buy it, nobody will do so. Why?

Clues: 238/Answer: 271.

Bags Away

An airplane nearly crashed because one of the passengers had not fastened his suitcase securely enough. What happened?

Clues: 227/Answer: 263.

The Unwelcome Guest

A couple had a neighbor who continually arrived at mealtimes in the hope of getting a free meal. How did they use their very friendly dog to persuade the neighbor not to come for free meals again?

Clues: 237/Answer: 270.

The Tallest Tree

Men found what they suspected was the tallest tree in Australia. It was growing in the outback in rough terrain and with other trees around. They did not have any advanced instruments with them. How did they accurately measure the height of the tree?

Clues: 236/Answer: 270.

Watch That Man!

A runner was awarded a prize for winning a marathon. But the judges disqualified him when they saw a picture of his wristwatch. Why?

Clues: 237/Answer: 271.

The Mighty Stone

There was a huge boulder in the middle of a village green. It was too big to be moved, too hard to split, and dynamiting it was too dangerous. How did a simple peasant suggest getting rid of it?

Clues: 232/Answer: 267.

The Fatal Fall

A woman dropped a piece of wood. She picked it up again and carried on as if nothing had happened. The wood was not damaged and she was not injured, but the incident cost her her life. Why?

Clues: 229-230/Answer: 264.

Election Selection

There is an election in a deprived city area. All the political parties put up candidates, actively canvass, and spend money on their campaigns. Yet the election is won by a candidate who did not canvass or advertise and is unknown to all of the electors. How?

Clues: 229/Answer: 264.

The Old Crooner

How did Bing Crosby reduce the crime rate in various U.S. cities?

Clues: 233/Answer: 267.

Generosity?

A man took considerable trouble to acquire some money, but then quickly gave most of it away. Why?

Clues: 230/Answer: 265.

The Sad Samaritan

Jim saw a stranded motorist on a country road. The motorist had run out of fuel, so Jim took him to the nearest garage and then drove him back to his car. Jim felt good that he had been such a good Samaritan, but discovered something later that made him very sad. What was it?

Clues: 235/Answer: 269.

HARD COME, EASY GO

PLAN "B" GET NEW MOTTO

Well Trained

A man, a woman, and a child are watching a train come into a station. "Here it comes," says the man. "Here she comes," says the woman. "Here he comes," says the child. Who was correct?

Clues: 238/Answer: 271.

Razor Attack

A man had his throat attacked by a woman with a razor, yet he suffered no serious injuries. How come?

Clues: 234/Answer: 268.

Critical Thinking Puzzles

Critical Thinking Puzzles

When we think critically we are engaging in intellectual strategies to probe the basic nature of a problem, situation, or puzzle. By these strategies, we mean making observations, predictions, generalizations, reasonings by assumptions, comparisons and contrasts, uncovering relationships between the parts to the whole, and looking for sequences. It sounds like a lot, but everyone has these skills and the puzzles in this book are designed to challenge, exercise, and stretch the way you interpret the world.

Some of the puzzles here are old favorites that have entertained people for years. Several of them are presented in their time-tested way. Most of the standards, however, have a new twist or updated story added. Other puzzles require some inventive solutions, so don't be afraid to be creative. Most of them can be done with pencil or pen.

Some require inexpensive material that can probably be found around the house: a pair of scissors, markers, tape, toothpicks, and a yardstick. Even though some puzzles can be solved using algebra, they were selected for their ability to be visualized and figured out this way. Therefore, in addition to being fun to do, they offer an arena to practice thinking skills.

Statements such as "I want you to memorize this list!" or "That's a good answer, but it wasn't the one I expected" help to extinguish critical thought. Although you'll never have to measure an ant's path or alter a flag, the process of creating and evaluating a reasonable answer is a worthwhile experience. By the time you finish this book, those powerful skills will be back on track, probing your everyday experiences for a more thorough and deeper understanding. Ready to start? Great, because the fun is about to begin.

Puzzle Paths

Sam Loyd was one of the most published and brilliant puzzle creators of all time. Born in 1841, Sam was an accomplished chess player by his early teens. He created puzzles based upon the moves of chess pieces. Loyd also produced thousands of other puzzles, many of which still appear today with contemporary twists and slight modifications. The maze below is based upon one of his earliest puzzle ideas. Can you complete the challenge?

The Amusing Amusement Park has three rides. It also has three gates with signs that identify the ride to which they lead. The only problem is that the architect forgot the layout of the connecting paths. Can you help? Draw three paths that connect the rides to their gates. The paths can't meet or cross.

Answer on page 283.

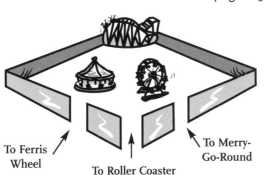

To Ferris Wheel

To Roller Coaster

To Merry-Go-Round

Turn, Turn, Turn

Ever heard of a multiaxial stimulator? Years ago, it appeared as a training device for astronauts and pilots. Nowadays, it's often found at beaches, amusement parks, and fairs. The MAS consists of three loops, each inside of the other. Each loop is free to rotate in only one dimension. The "pilot" is fastened to the middle of the innermost loop. In this position, a person gets to experience all three turning motions at the same time.

Let's strap the number "4" in this simulator. Suppose each of the loops made one half rotation. How would the "4" appear after it was flipped, turned, and spun halfway in all three dimensions? You can select from the choices below.

Answer on page 286.

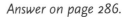

a. ⊬ b. ⊹ c. ⊬ d. 4 e. ⊣ f. ⊣

Mind Bend

According to Einstein, in some places the shortest distance between two points is not a straight line! Consider this: In space, the gravitational field of huge objects is strong enough to warp space. In these curved dimensions, the concept represented by a straight line bends to fit the framework of the distorted space. Mind bending, huh?

Here's another type of mind bender. The shape below is made from a single index card. No section of the card has been removed or taped back in place. Can you duplicate its appearance using several snips of a scissors? Have fun!

Answer on page 282.

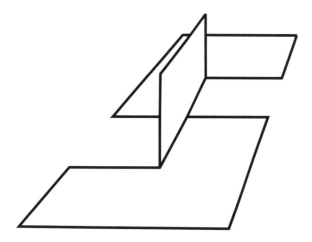

Whale of a Problem

In spite of their name, killer whales don't hunt and kill people. In fact, these dolphin-like animals prefer to eat smaller marine animals, such as seals and penguins. Biologists believe that rare attacks on humans occur because of misidentification. Obscured by daylight or icebergs, the image of a person may be mistaken for that of a penguin from below.

Now here's the problem. Acting alone, it takes two killer whales 2 minutes to catch two seals. Based upon this rate, how long will it take a pod of ten killer whales to catch ten seals?

Answer on page 287.

Main Attraction

Like all magnets, a bar magnet has a North and South Pole. At each of these poles, the magnetic force is the strongest. It is powerful enough to attract and repel iron objects. Near the middle of the magnet, however, the force is hardly detectable.

Suppose you have two identical iron bars. Only one of the bars has been magnetized. Suppose you can only pick up and manipulate one bar of these two bars. How can you tell if it is the magnetized or unmagnetized bar?

Answer on page 281.

Runaway Runway

"Good afternoon. This is your captain speaking. We're fourth in line for departure. As soon as these four albatross birds take off, we'll begin our flight. Thank you for your patience."

Strange, but true. Pilots must sometimes compete with birds for runway usage. The same physical principles that lift an aircraft into the sky are at work in our feathered friends. Runways that are constructed to offer better lifting conditions for aircrafts inadvertently produce great takeoff locations for birds.

Speaking of runways, here's our puzzle. If an airport has three separate runways, there can be a maximum of three intersections. Suppose there are four runways. What is the maximum number of possible intersections?

Answer on page 284.

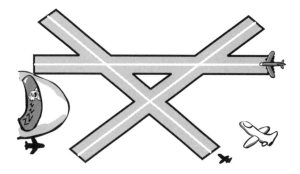

Raises and Cuts

Like many modern-day products, paper toweling arose from a factory mistake. A mill-sized roll of paper that should have been cut and packaged into soft bathroom tissue was manufactured thick and wrinkled. Instead of junking the roll, the workers perforated the unattractive paper into towel-sized sheets. And so, the paper towel was born.

Several years ago, Moe and Bo began work at a paper towel factory. At the end of the first week, the owner evaluated both workers. Pleased with Moe, she increased his weekly wage by 10%. Disappointed with Bo, she cut her salary by 10%. The following week, the owner decided to make their salaries more equal. To do so, she cut Moe's new salary by 10%. At the same time, she increased Bo's salary by 10%. Now, which worker earned more?

Answer on page 283-284.

The Race Is On

The material we call rubber is another product of a mishap in the kitchen! Prior to the mid-1800s, rubber was a troublesome material. In the summer heat, it became soft and sticky. In the winter cold, it became hard and brittle. In searching for a way to improve the properties of rubber, Charles Goodyear accidentally spilled a spoonful of a rubber and sulfur mixture onto his stove. When he later examined the solidified spill, he uncovered a flexible material that could withstand heat and cold.

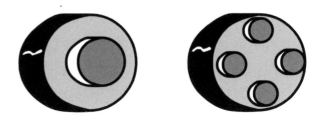

Take a look at the two solid rubber wheels below. Both have been modified by retired ice skaters. On the first wheel, 4 pounds of lead are positioned in one central lump. On the second wheel, the same amount of lead is spread out into four 1-pound lumps so that they are positioned closer to the wheel's rim.

Suppose these wheels are released down identical inclines. If we don't consider air resistance, will these wheels accelerate at the same rate?

Answer on page 285.

Screwy Stuff

Take a close look at the two screws below. Suppose they were both turned in a counterclockwise rotation. What will happen to each screw?

Answer on page 284.

Screws in the Head

The pitch made by a vibrating string is dependent upon several factors, including the tension in the string. The more tightly pulled (greater tension), the higher the pitch. Likewise, if the string is relaxed (less tension), it produces a note of lower pitch. Many guitars have a screw-like arrangement that varies the tension in the individual strings. As the tuner head is turned, this movement is transferred to a post. The turn of the post changes the tension in its wrapped string to produce a note of different pitch.

Take a look at the tuning heads below. What happens to the pitch of the sound when the head is rotated in a clockwise manner?

Answer on page 284.

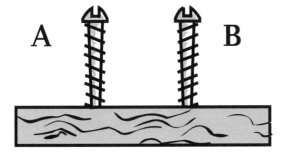

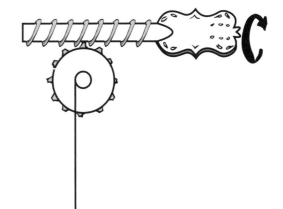

Change of Pace

Here are several puzzles that use a handful of change.

Consider this: I have ten coins in my pocket. The value of these coins is 50 cents. How many coins of each denomination are there?

Okay, so that one wasn't too difficult. How about finding the identity of thirty coins whose value is $1.00?

Answer on page 278.

Spiral^2

While exploring the ruins of an ancient city, an archaeologist uncovers an odd structure. The structure is made of stone walls that form a square spiral. The sides of the outside spiral measure 100 feet X 100 feet. The path throughout the entire structure is 2 feet wide.

If the archeologist walks along the exact center of the path, how far will he travel from the entrance to the end of the spiral?

Answer on page 285.

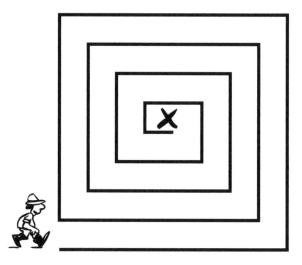

Take 'em Away

This arrangement of toothpicks forms fourteen different squares of various sizes. Can you remove six toothpicks and leave only three squares behind?

Answer on page 286.

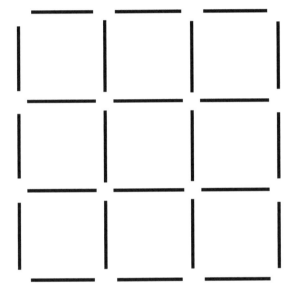

Get Set. Go!

Two cyclists race along a straight course. The faster of the pair maintains an average speed of 30 mph. The slower cyclist averages 25 miles per hour. When the race ends, the judges announce that the faster cyclist crossed the finish line one hour before the slower racer. How many miles long was the racing course?

Answer on pages 279.

Don't Stop Now

Now that you are familiar with the pattern, let's try one more removal problem. Starting with the same twenty-four toothpick grid, remove eight toothpicks and leave exactly three squares behind.

Answer on page 279.

Coin Roll

Run your fingernail around the rim of a dime or quarter and you'll feel a series of small ridges. These ridges appeared on coins hundreds of years ago. At that time, many coins were made out of silver and other valuable metals. To prevent people from "shaving" the metal from the edge of the coin (and selling the metal shavings), telltale ridges were added to the coin's rim. If a coin's edge was cut away, the telltale ridges would be lost.

In this problem, we'll use those ridges to prevent the coins from slipping. Consider two dimes within a track formed by parallel chopsticks. Although the coins can move, their snug fit makes both coins move at the same time. Therefore, if we were to rotate one of the dimes, the other would spin at the same speed but in the opposite direction. This results in both dimes moving along the track and maintaining their relative head-to-head position. Suppose, however, we change our

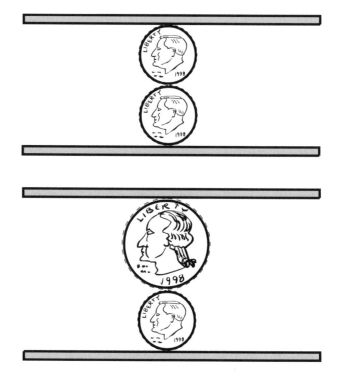

setup and replace one of the dimes with a quarter. If the quarter is rotated along the track, how would its head-to-head position with the smaller dime change?

Answer on page 278.

More Coinage

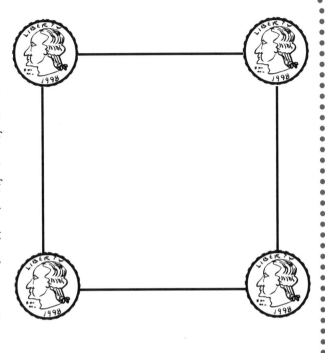

The four coins are positioned at the corners of a square. The side length of this square (measured from the center of each coin) is 8 inches. Here's the challenge. Can you change the positions of only two coins so that so that the new square formed by the coin arrangement has a side length slightly more than 5¹/2 inches?

Answer on page 282.

Some Things Never Change

People have written down puzzles for nearly 5000 years. One of the first puzzle collections was recorded about 1650 b.c. on a scroll called the Rhind papyrus. The word Rhind comes from the name Henry Rhind, a Scottish archaeologist who explored Egypt. Papyrus is a paper-like material that was used as a writing tablet by the ancient Egyptians.

The Rhind papyrus is a scroll that is over 18 feet long and about a foot wide.

It was written on both sides by a person named Ahmes. Roughly translated (and somewhat updated), one of the puzzles from the scroll is presented below.

There are seven houses, each containing seven cats. Each cat kills seven mice, and each mouse would have eaten seven ears of corn. Each ear of corn would have produced seven sacks of grain. What is the total number of all of these items?

Answer on page 285.

Doing Wheelies

The outer rim of each "double wheel" is twice the diameter of the wheel's inner rim. Suppose the top wheel rotates at ten revolutions per second. At what speed will wheel A and wheel B spin?

Answer on page 279.

More Wheelies

The outermost rim of these wheels is twice the diameter of the middle rim. The middle rim is twice the diameter of the innermost rim. Suppose wheel A rotates at sixteen revolutions per second. How many revolutions will wheel C complete in a minute?

Answer on page 283.

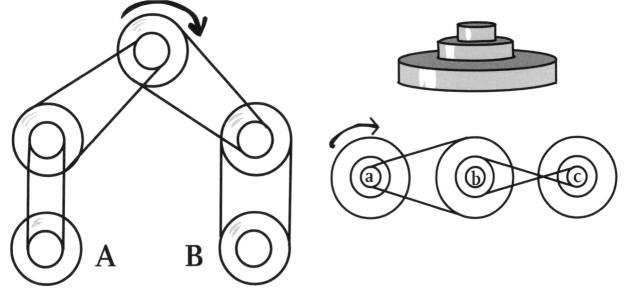

Good Guess

In order to win a free visit to the dentist, students had to guess the exact number of gumballs in a fish bowl. The students guessed 45, 41, 55, 50, and 43, but no one won. The guesses were off by 3, 7, 5, 7, and 2 (in no given order). From this information, determine the number of gumballs in the bowl.

Answer on page 280.

Check It Out

The six sections below are parts of a 5 x 5 checkerboard grid. Can you piece them back together to form the original pattern?

Answer on page 278.

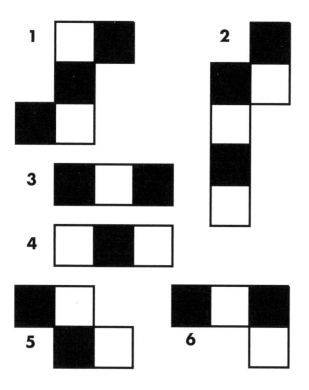

Oops, I Wasn't Concentrating

A pitcher is filled to the brim with grape juice. While raiding the refrigerator, Anthony accidentally knocks the pitcher over so that half of the contents spill out. Hoping no one will notice, Anthony adds tap water to the half-filled pitcher, bringing the volume of the diluted juice to the top. He then pours himself a glass of the watered down juice, leaving the pitcher three-fourths full.

"Yuck! This needs more flavor!" he exclaims and then adds more grape flavor by filling the pitcher to the brim with double-strength grape juice.

How does the concentration of this final solution compare with the original grape drink?

Answer on page 283.

106

Bridge, Anyone?

Ever heard of Galloping Girdie? If not, perhaps you've seen an old science fiction movie that showed a clip of a large suspension bridge twisting apart and falling into the river below it. That was Galloping Girdie.

It spanned a large river in the state of Washington. Soon after it was constructed, people noticed that winds would cause the bridge to sway and shake. During one incident of heavy winds, the bridge shook so violently that it fell apart into the river below. Bye-bye, Girdie.

Now, it's your turn to design a bridge. To build it, you'll need three ice cream sticks. If you don't have these sticks, you can use three pieces of stiff cardboard. The cardboard sections should be $4\frac{1}{2}$ inches long and $\frac{1}{2}$ inch wide.

Position three cups in a triangular pattern. The cups should be placed so that the edge-to-edge distance between any two of the cups is 5 inches.

Hmm... 5-inch canyons, but only $4\frac{1}{2}$-inch bridges. Your job is to construct a bridge using these three pieces and span the gaps connecting all three cups.

Answer on page 278.

Face Lift

Take a look at the shape below. Although it is made up of four identical cubes, you can only see three of them. The fourth cube is hidden in the bottom back-corner. Imagine picking the shape up and examining it from all angles. How many different cube faces can you count?

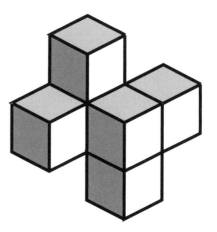

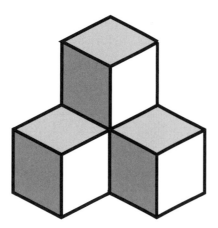

Okay, so it wasn't that hard. Try this one. The "double L" shape is made up of six cubes. The sixth cube is hidden in the back of the middle layer. If you could examine the stack from all angles, how many faces would you see?

Okay, okay, okay. Here's one more. This one consists of only five cubes. Actually it

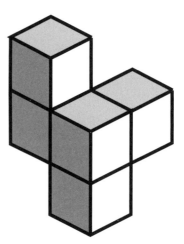

resembles the "double L" shape, except that one of the cubes is removed.

Answer on page 279.

Trying Times

The triangle below is divided into four equal parts. Suppose you can paint one or more of these four smaller parts black. How many different and distinguishable patterns (including the pattern which has no painted triangles) can you form?

Remember, each pattern must be unique and not be duplicated by simply rotating the large figure.

Answer on page 286.

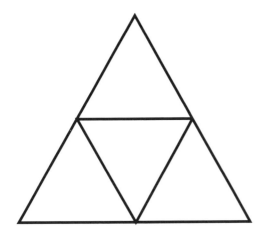

Weighty Problem

Did you know that during periods of weightlessness, astronauts lose bone mass? To prevent any serious loss, people in space must exercise. Stressing and stretching body parts help keep bone material from being reabsorbed into the body.

For a moment, let's imagine our weightless astronaut returning to Earth. She steps onto a scale and weighs herself. When the lab assistant asks her for her weight, she offers an obscure (but challenging) answer.

"According to this scale, I weigh 60 pounds plus half my weight."

Can you figure out how much this puzzling space traveler weighs?

Answer on pages 287.

Number Blocks

Take a look at the three stacks of numbered blocks below. Can you rearrange the blocks by exchanging one (and only one) from each of the three stacks so that the sum of the numbers in each stack is equal to the sum of numbers in either other stack?

Answer on page 283.

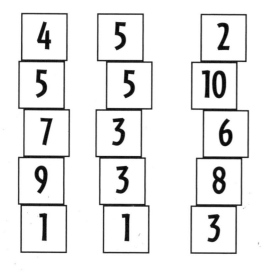

Separation Anxiety

Using three straight lines, separate the apples from the oranges.

Answer on page 285.

Give Me Five

How many 5's are in the number 5555?

Answer on page 280.

Breaking Up Is Hard to Do... Sometimes

Take a look at the square and triangle below. Both figures are divided into four equal and identical parts so that each part has the same shape of the original figure (only smaller).

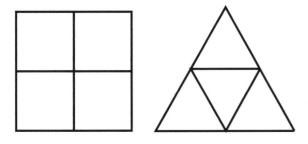

So far, so good. Now try to divide the figure below into four equal and identical parts, each with the same shape as the original figure.

Answer on page 277.

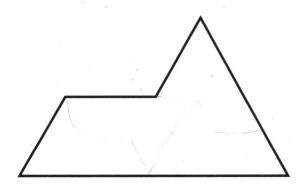

Mind Slice

Close your eyes and imagine a perfect sphere. Now, imagine a cleaver placed at a point anywhere on the surface of the sphere. How does changing the angle of the cleaver slice affect the shape of the exposed faces?

Answer on page 282.

Satellite Surveyor

Satellites that orbit the Earth can see all sorts of things. Spy satellites, for example, have lenses that are powerful enough to "read" license plate numbers on cars. Other types of satellites can "look beneath" the Earth's surface. Some of these images have been used to uncover lost civilizations that have been buried for thousands of years under shifting desert sands.

In this problem, we'll use our satellite to help survey a plot of land.

The basic plot is a square that measures 20 miles on a side. Suppose the midpoint of each side is used as a marker to divide the entire plot into nine plots of various sizes and shapes. Without performing any higher math magic (just stick to plain ol' logic, with a little geometry), what is the area of the shaded central square?

NOTE: Before you bask in premature glory, it is not equal to 100 square miles!

Answer on page 284.

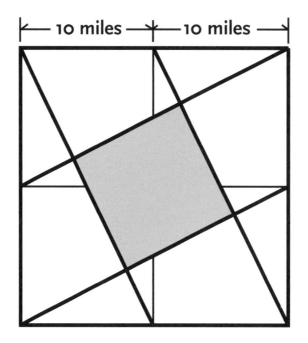

← 10 miles → ← 10 miles →

Say Cheese

The total surface area of any cube is equal to the sum of the surface areas of each of the six sides. For example, the cheese cube below measures 2 inches on each side. Therefore, the surface area of each side equals 2 inches x 2 inches, or 4 square inches. Since there are six sides, the total surface area of this cube is 24 square inches.

Now, the challenge. Using as many cuts as needed, divide this cube into pieces whose surface area sum is twice the surface area of this 2 x 2 cube.

Answer on page 284.

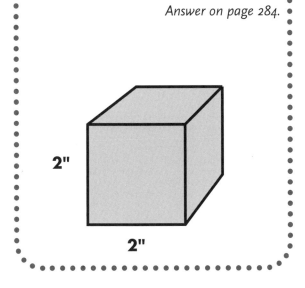

Magic Star

For those of you who are tired of magic squares and magic triangles, may we present The Magic Star? In this puzzle, you'll have to use the numbers one through twelve. Only one number can be placed in a circle, and all the numbers must be used. When placed correctly, the sum of all rows of four must be the same.

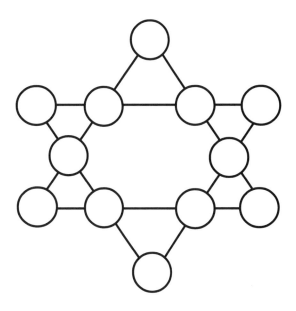

HINT: All of the side sums equal twenty-six.

Answer on page 281.

Keep on Tickin'

Divide the face of a watch into three sections. The sum of the numbers included on each section must equal the sum of the numbers on either of the other two sections. Let's not waste any time—the clock is ticking.

Answer on pages 280.

ARE YOU SURE YOU READ THE PROBLEM CORRECTLY?

Going Batty

Click, click, click, click. Like submarines, bats have a sonar system called echolocation. They use their echolocation to find objects. The clicking sounds made by bats move outward like the beam of a lighthouse. When the sounds strike an object (such as an insect meal), they are reflected back to the bat's large ears. With incredible speed, the bat's brain analyzes the echo return time and uses it to accurately locate the target's position.

Now, let's put that echolocation to work. Over a five-night period, a bat targets and captures a total of a hundred beetles. During each night, the bat captured six more beetles than on the previous night. How many beetles did the bat catch on each night?

Answer on page 280.

Cards, Anyone?

Use a pair of scissors to carefully cut out two unequal corners of an index card as shown below. Can you now use the scissors to cut this modified card into two identical halves?

NOTE: The identical halves must be formed without flipping either piece over.

Let's keep up the cutting challenge. Copy the pattern below onto an index card. Use your scissors to trim off the excess card stock. Now, here's the challenge. Divide this shape into four equal and identical parts that can fit back together to form a perfect square.

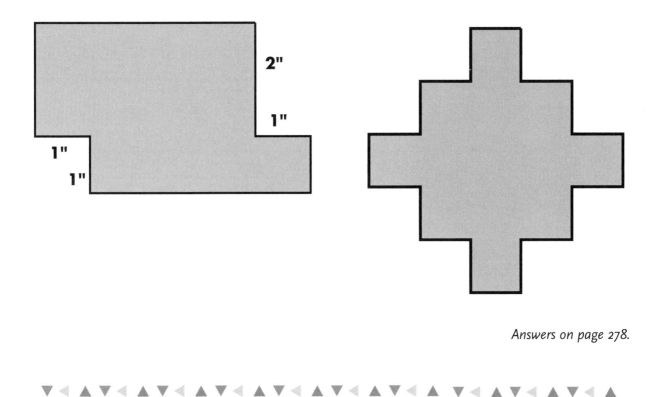

Answers on page 278.

Sequence Grid

A sequence grid is formed by items that are related by their order. Here are two examples. As you can see, the placement of the numbers and letters reflects a sequence.

The first square is filled in an order based on dividing a number in half. The second square illustrates a sequence of letters that is separated by single (but not recorded) middle letters.

512	256	128
64	32	16
8	4	2

A	C	E
G	I	K
M	O	Q

Now that you know what a sequence grid is, here's one to sharpen your puzzling skills on.

Answer on page 285.

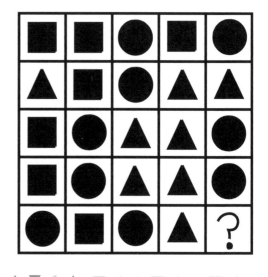

Breaking the Rules

A ruler is placed on two pieces of chalk as shown below. As the ruler is pushed, it moves 4 inches ahead. How far did either one of the chalk pieces roll?

Answer on page 277.

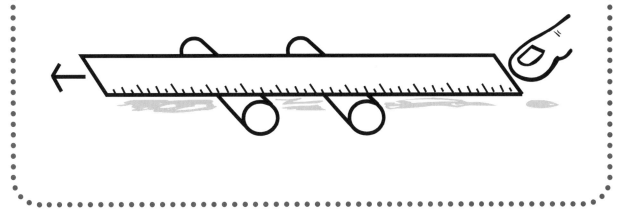

Balance

Suppose you have a balance and a 2-gram and 5-gram mass. How can the balance be used only three times to separate 80 grams of fat into piles of 13 grams and 67 grams?

Answer on page 277.

Togetherness

A computer and its monitor weigh a total of 48 pounds. If the monitor weighs twice as much as the computer, how much does each piece of hardware weigh?

Answer on page 286.

Big Magic

The figure below is called a magic square. Do you see why it's called magic? The sum of any three-box side (and the two three-box diagonals) is equal to the sum of any other side (or diagonal). In this case, they are all equal to fifteen.

The sections belong to a four-by-four magic square. Your job is to assemble these sections into a complete sixteen-box magic square. To do so, you'll first have to uncover the sum of the side for this figure.

8	3	4
1	5	9
6	7	2

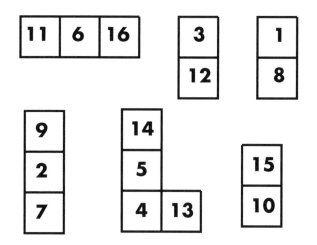

Answer on page 277.

Look Over Here

Note the direction in which each eye looks. Can you uncover the pattern? Good. Now find the empty eye. In which direction should this eye be looking?

Answer on page 281.

Time on Your Hands

Examine the series of three clock-faces shown below. When you uncover the pattern of the hand movement, select from the choice of times that will be closest to what the fourth clock should read.

Answer on page 286.

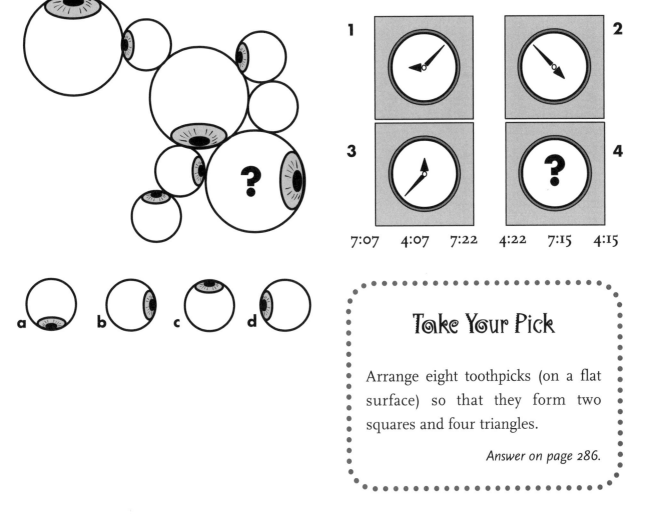

7:07   4:07   7:22   4:22   7:15   4:15

Take Your Pick

Arrange eight toothpicks (on a flat surface) so that they form two squares and four triangles.

Answer on page 286.

One Way Only

Can you trace the following figure using only one continuous line? Place your pencil anywhere on the figure. Then, draw the rest of the figure without lifting your pencil from the page.

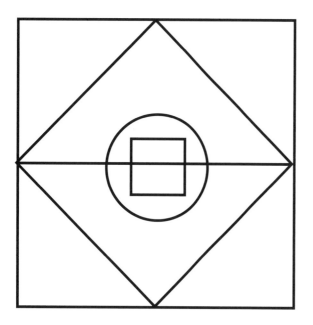

NOTE: This line cannot cross over itself nor retrace any part of its path.

Answer on page 283.

Lasagna Cut

A square pan filled with piping-hot lasagna is set aside to cool. When the hungry chefs return, they discover that a quarter of the lasagna has mysteriously disappeared (as shown below). Frustrated, they decide to divide the remaining piece into four equal portions before any more is eaten. All cuts must be normal—no slicing through the plane of the surface allowed. What is the cutting pattern that will meet the needs of these chefs?

HINT: The simplest solution requires cutting this meal into eight pieces and supplying each person with two smaller pieces.

Answer on pages 281.

Iron Horse Race

Two trains race against each other on parallel tracks. The Casey Jones Special is a coal-fed steam engine that travels at a respectable speed. The newer, oil-burning Metropolitan Diesel travels $1\frac{1}{2}$ times the speed of The Casey Jones Special. To make the race a closer competition, The Casey Jones Special begins the race $1\frac{1}{2}$ hours before its opponent. How long will it take the Metropolitan Diesel to catch up to the slower steam engine?

Answer on page 280.

Thick as a Brick

If the chimney below is complete on all four sides, how many bricks does the whole structure contain?

Answer on page 286.

Here, Art, Art, Art

How quickly can you uncover the perfect five-pointed star hidden in the design below?

Answer on page 280.

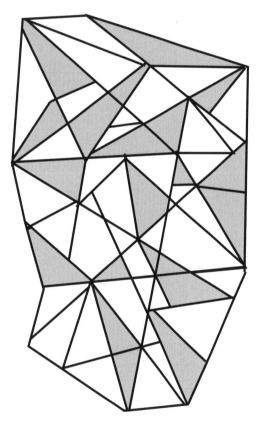

Surrounded By Squares

How many squares can you uncover in the pattern below? Don't forget to count the outer border as one of your answers!

Answer on page 286.

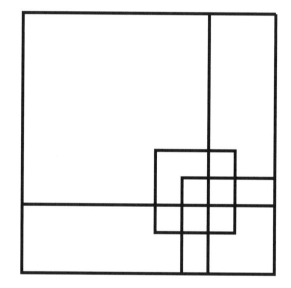

More Cheese

A grocer has a large cube of cheese that she wishes to divide into twenty-seven smaller and equal-sized cubes. To cut out the twenty-seven blocks, she uses two cuts to divide the cube into three slices. She stacks these slices atop of each other and makes two more cuts. Finally, she rotates the cube a quarter-turn and makes the final cut. The result is twenty-seven identical cubes made with six cuts. Is it possible to get the twenty-seven cubes with fewer cuts? If so, how?

Answer on page 282.

Break It Up!

If you look carefully, you'll be able to uncover thirty squares in the toothpick pattern below. Your challenge is to find the fewest number of toothpicks that, when removed, leaves no complete square pattern intact.

Answer on page 277.

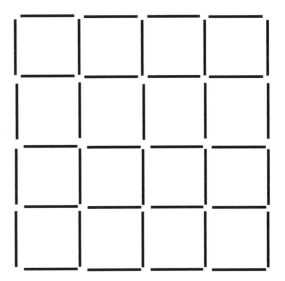

Exactly... Well, Almost

Which of the designs below is unlike the other five?

Answer on page 279.

Parts of a Whole

Copy the five shapes shown below onto a separate sheet of paper. Use a pair of scissors to carefully cut out the shapes. Here's the challenge. Arrange them to form a triangle whose three sides are of equal length.

Answer on page 283.

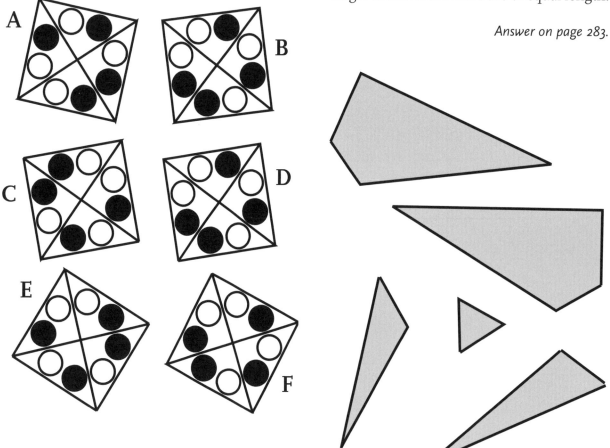

A Game for Losers

The object of this modified game of tic-tac-toe is to lose! In order to win, you must force your opponent to complete three squares in a row. Let's enter a game that has already been started. You are "O" and it is your turn. In which box or boxes should you place your "O" marker to ensure that you win by losing (no matter where your opponent goes)?

Answer on page 279.

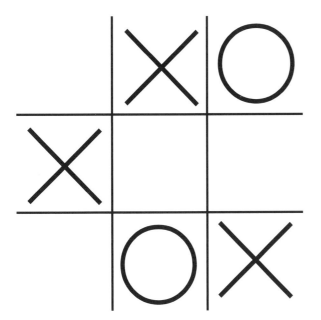

Roller Coaster, Roll!

Ed and his identical twin brother Ed build roller coaster tracks. They've just completed two hills that are both 40 feet high. As you can see, the slopes of the two hills are somewhat different. Ed (the older twin) rides a car that will travel along on a straight slope. Ed (the younger twin) rides a car that will travel along a curved slope. If both cars are released at the exact same time, which Ed will arrive at the bottom of this slope first?

Answer on page 284.

Sum Puzzle

Copy the pattern and numbers shown below onto a sheet of paper. Then carefully use a pair of scissors to separate the sheet into nine separate squares. Rebuild the larger square using the following strategy. The sum of any two adjacent numbers must equal ten. Have fun.

Answer on page 285.

A Class Act

There are thirty students in a class. Five of these students do not play any sort of musical instrument. Among the others, eighteen students play guitar. Six of these guitar players also play keyboards. How many of students in the class play only keyboards?

Answer on page 278.

I WILL NOW PLAY FOR YOU THE MINUTE WALTZ IN 30 SECONDS

Cool Cut

Shut your eyes and try to imagine a perfect ice cube. If you're good at visualizing, you may be able to "see" the edges and faces that are positioned on the far side of the cube. Good. Now, here's the challenge. With one cut, how can you divide this cube so that a perfect triangular face is exposed? Don't forget, a regular triangle has all three sides of equal length.

Answer on page 279.

Melt Down

Unlike most liquids, water freezes into a solid that is less dense than its former liquid state. Since it is less dense, ice floats in water. At the surface, the ice acts as an insulator to help trap heat within the water below. This layer of frozen insulation actually insulates lakes, rivers, ponds, and oceans from freezing into a complete solid.

Now let's bring this information back to the kitchen. An ice cube floats freely in a glass filled to the brim with water. Will the water level rise or sink as the ice cube melts?

Answer on page 282.

...at's the Angle?

...al triangle has three sides that are a... ...ual length. This familiar shape can be constructed from three identical pieces. Examine the shapes below. Which of these shapes illustrates this building block? Once you've selected the shape, make three copies of it on a separate sheet of paper. Cut out and arrange these pieces so that they form an equilateral triangle.

Answer on page 287.

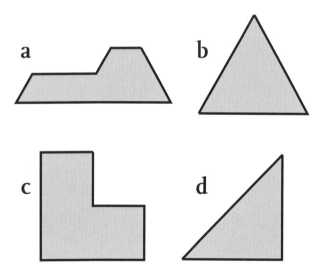

a

b

c

d

Here, Spot, Spot, Spot

Without lifting your pencil from the paper, draw six straight lines that connect all sixteen of the dots below. To make things more of a challenge, the line pattern that you create must begin at the "x".

Answer on page 280.

X

128

Keeping Time

The strike of a lightning bolt can create a tremendous surge of electricity. If this electric flow reaches the delicate circuits of a computer, it can "burn out" the sensitive components. To prevent against this damage, computers are plugged into surge protectors, which stop the electric flow if a damaging level of electricity is detected.

In this problem, there are no surge protectors. Two electronic clocks are plugged directly into the wall socket. A surge of electricity flows through both clocks and affects their time-keeping circuits. One clock is now 5 minutes per hour fast. The other clock is now 5 minutes per hour slow. In how many hours will the clocks be exactly one hour apart?

Answer on page 280.

129

Wrap It Up

You are about to engage your intellect in quite an interesting challenge.

Did you know that fortune cookies didn't originate in China? They were created in the U.S. by the owner of an Asian restaurant who wished to amuse his customers while they waited for their meals to be cooked. Over time, fortune cookies evolved into a treat that is now offered at the end of the meal. That's a wrap. And speaking of wraps...

Take a look at the steps in which the cookie wrapper below was folded. In the final step, two holes were punched through the layers of the folds.

Now unroll this wrapper. Which of the patterns would it resemble?

Answer on page 287.

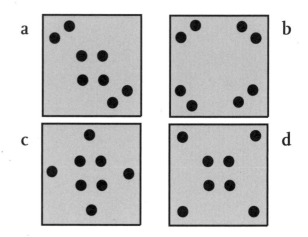

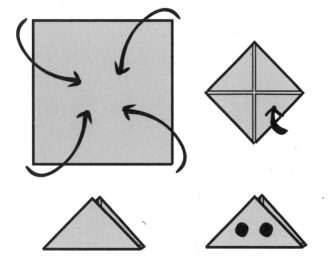

Pyramid Passage

Ancient Egyptian pyramids were built as royal tombs. Within these massive stone structures were rooms, halls, and connecting passageways. Look at the figure below. Can you draw four paths that connect the matching symbols? The paths may not cross, nor may they go outside the large pyramid boundary.

Answer on page 287.

Magic Pyramid

For this pyramid, can you place the numbers 1,2,3,4,5, and 6 in the circles shown below? Only one number may be placed in a circle and all numbers must be used. When the final arrangement is complete, the sum of each side's three numbers must all be the same number.

Answer on page 287.

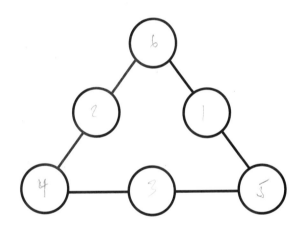

Pyramid Builders

The Egyptian pyramids at Giza are incredible structures that took many years to complete. They were constructed out of large rectangular stone blocks, each weighing about as much as a car. The two largest pyramids contain over two million of these blocks!

Now, it's your turn to work. Can you build a three dimensional pyramid using two odd-shaped blocks?

Copy the figure below onto two pieces of stiff paper. Fold along the inner lines as shown and use tape to secure the edges.

Now arrange the pentahedron blocks to form a tetrahedron pyramid.

Answer on page 288.

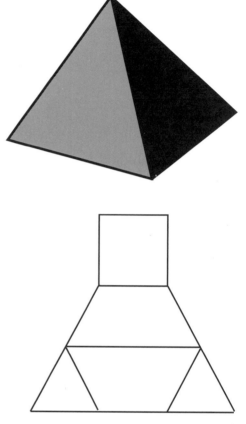

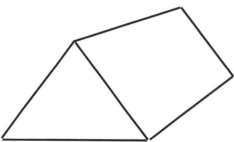

Trial by Triangle

Take a look at these two identical triangles. They are made with six sticks.
Can you rearrange the sticks so that they form four triangles? All of the new triangles must be the same size as these original two!

Answer on page 288.

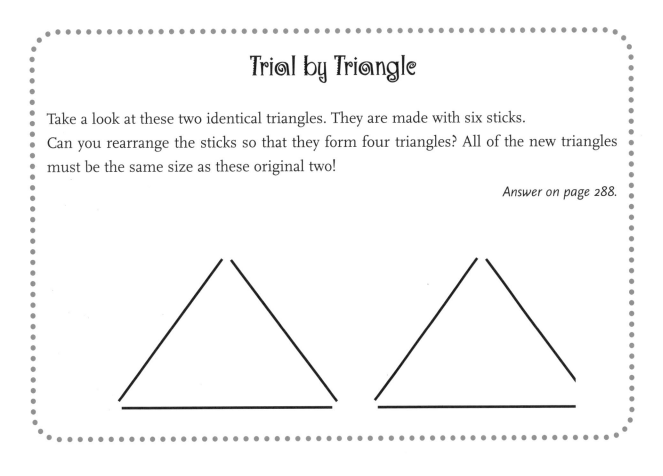

Trapezoid 2 Triangle

Here's another triangle whose only problem is that it isn't built yet. You'll have to assemble it from these three trapezoids!

Answer on page 288.

By the way, here's a triangle that you can draw but can't build. It's called an impossible triangle. See why?

Before you go on to the next puzzle, take at look at these strange objects. Do you think that they can also be built? Or do you think there may be some sort of trick?

Answer on page 288.

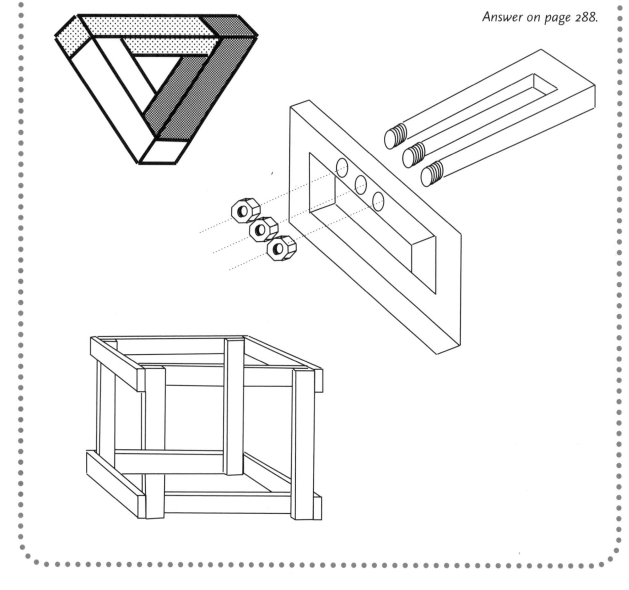

Spare My Brain

To move their armies, the Romans built over 50,000 miles of roads. Imagine driving all those miles! Now imagine driving those miles in the first gasoline-driven car that has only three wheels and could reach a top speed of about 10 miles per hour.

For safety's sake, let's bring along a spare tire. As you drive the 50,000 miles, you rotate the spare with the other tires so that all four tires get the same amount of wear. Can you figure out how many miles of wear each tire accumulates?

Answer on page 288.

Whirling Paradox

Let's take a closer look at those tires. If a car with spoke wheels drives by, we will see that when the spinning spokes get to the top of the wheel, they are moving so fast that they become blurred. At the same time, the spokes on the bottom half of the wheel appear to be moving much slower. In fact, they are so slow that you may be able to count them. If the spokes are connected to the same wheel, how can this be?

HINT: There may be a connection between this observation and the sound of a speeding car as it zooms by.

Answer on page 288.

Lost?

Now we're on foot. Imagine that you and several friends have hiked into a remote region of the countryside. Your final destination is the land of Ultima. After leaving the village of Skullara, you continue following the trail and come across an important intersection. There is, however, one slight problem.

The sign showing which way to go has been knocked down. How can you figure out what is the right direction you need to go?

Answer on page 288.

Answer on page 288.

Compass Caper

A compass is a reliable tool that always points north—or does it? There are many reports of compass needles that unexpectedly turn away from north. The strangest natural cause for this disturbance may be a shooting star. As the meteor streaks across the sky, it upsets the electrical balance of the air and produces a magnetic force that some believe effects the compass reading.

We, however, will work with a compass that always gives a true heading. Suppose you start a hike by traveling directly south for 500 paces. Then, you turn and go due east for another 100 paces. You turn once more and go due north for 500 paces. You are now back where you started from, but in front of you is a bear. What color is it?

Answer on page 289.

Answer on page 289.

Sand Traps

As you continue on your hike, you're handed a map of the terrain ahead. This is not a safe place. In fact, the entire region is filled with quicksand, which is shown on the map as black splotches. Contrary to belief, quicksand does not suck or pull you under. Instead, it's your weight that makes you sink in this water and fine sand mixture.

Your challenge is to discover a path from any point on the bottom edge of the map to any point on the top edge without running into quicksand (black splotches). To make it more challenging, the path must consist of only two straight lines.

To start, place your pencil anywhere on the bottom border of the map. Then draw a straight line. When you stop, don't lift the pencil. Complete your trip using one more straight line.

Answer on page 288.

Which Mountain?

Now that you've made it past the quicksand, it's time to do some climbing. You have a choice of climbing one of three geometrically shaped mountains, which are all 10,000 feet high. One of the mountains is a perfect cylinder, another is in the shape of a cone, and the third looks like the top half of a sphere. Several out-of-work math teachers have constructed roads that go from the base to the summit of each mountain. All three roads are built so that you climb 1 vertical foot every 20 horizontal feet. If you wish to walk the shortest distance from base to summit, which mountain would you choose?

Answer on page 289.

A Cut Above

With all that hiking, you've probably now worked up an appetite. So how about some pizza?

Suppose this is the early 1900s and you're in New York City's Little Italy getting a Pizza Margherita, named in honor of a pizza-loving Italian princess. Can you divide the pie into eight equal slices in only three straight cuts? All the pieces must be identical: each with an upper surface covered with sauce, lower baked crust, and a crusty edge.

HINT: Don't worry about the mess. You won't have to clean it.

Answer on page 289.

Kitchen Cups

Have you ever seen the written form of the Sanskrit language? If so, you probably are amazed at how different this ancient language from India looks from ours. Some English words, however, are based on Sanskrit. For example, cup comes from the Sanskrit word kupa, which means water well. This puzzle requires several water wells.

Suppose you need to measure exactly 1 cup of water. All that you have in your kitchen are two containers. The smaller container holds 3 cups and the larger holds 5 cups. How can you use these two containers to measure exactly 1 cup of water?

Answer on page 289.

Moldy Math

Now let's talk about something else that you might have, but not want, in your kitchen. While you are raiding the refrigerator, you look behind the stove and discover a slice of bread that you misplaced several weeks ago. Needless to say, it is covered with mold. Since the mold started growing, the area it has covered has doubled each day. By the end of the eighth day, the entire surface of the bread is covered. When was the bread half-covered with mold?

Answer on page 289.

139

And a Cut Below

Have you ever heard of the cheesemobile? It's a giant refrigerated truck that was built to carry a piece of Cheddar cheese. Why, then, all the fuss? Simple. The cheese weighed over 40,000 pounds!

Take a look at the smaller barrel of cheese below. If you make these three complete and straight cuts, how many pieces of cheese will you have?

Answer on page 289.

Egg Exactly

Suppose you have only two egg timers, a 5-minute and a 3-minute. Can you use these two measuring devices to time an egg that must be boiled for exactly 2 minutes?

Answer on page 289.

Losing Marbles?

Marbles have been around for a long time. In fact, archaeologists have discovered marbles buried alongside an Egyptian child who died over 4000 years ago! The word "marble," however, comes from the Greek word marmaros, which is a white polished stone made from the mineral agate.

Now it's your turn to play with them. Place a marble in a cup and carry it to the opposite side of the room. Too easy, huh? To make this more challenging, the cup must be turned upside down. This may take a little bit of creative problem solving, but it can be done.

Answer on page 289.

A Puzzle of Portions

Did you know that 3 ounces plus 3 ounces doesn't always equal 6 ounces? As illogical as this may sound, its true because of the behavior of the small particles (and spaces) that make up liquids. When different liquids are mixed, the particles tend to fill in some of the open spaces. As a result, the liquid becomes more compact and occupies less volume. It's only a small difference, but it is measurable.

Let's try mixing something whose volume does not change. Your challenge is to split some apple juice into three equal portions. The juice comes in a 24-ounce container. You have only three other containers, each holding 5, 11, and 13 ounces. How can you divide the juice into three equal portions?

HINT: At the very least, it will take four steps.

Answer on page 290.

Mixed Up?

Root beer, not cola, is the oldest-marketed soft drink in America. Before it was sold in the United States, root beer was brewed in many colonial homes. It contained many ingredients including molasses, licorice, vanilla, and the bark from birch trees. It was going to be called root tea but was later changed to root beer to attract the tavern crowd.

Here is one 8-ounce cup filled with root beer and another 8-ounce cup filled with cola. Take 1 tablespoon of root beer and add it to the cola. Stir the mixture. Now take 1 tablespoon of the mixture and add it to the root beer. Is there more root beer in the cola or cola in the root beer?

Answer on page 290.

Toothpick Teasers

For the puzzles in this group, you can also use pieces of straws or small sticks if you don't have toothpicks.

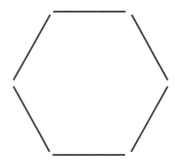

These six toothpicks are arranged in a hexagon. Starting with this arrangement, can you form two identical diamonds by moving only two toothpicks and adding just one more?

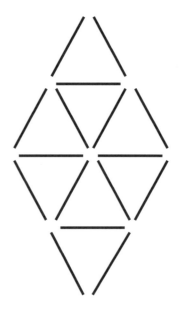

These sixteen toothpicks form eight identical triangles. Can you remove four toothpicks so that four of these triangles are left? All of the toothpicks that remain must be a side of the triangles with no loose ends sticking out.

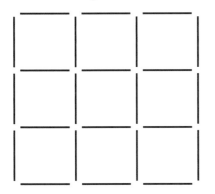

Form four (and only four) identical squares by removing eight toothpicks.

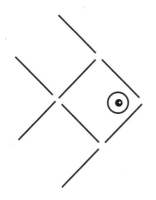

Move only three of the toothpicks (and the eye) to make the fish swim in the opposite direction.

Answers on pages 290.

Going to the Movies

Let's take a break from these puzzles and go to the movies. The map below shows an assortment of routes from your home (H) to the movie theater (M).

If you can only to travel in a north, east, or northeast direction, how many possible routes are there from your home to the theater?

Answer on page 290.

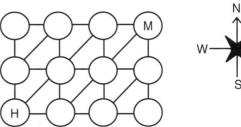

Weighing In...

The movie playing in the theater is about a scientist who changes into a fly. Before she transforms herself, she carefully weighs a jar of sleeping flies. Then, she shakes the jar to wake them up. While they are flying, the scientist weighs the jar again. Does the jar full of flies weigh less when the insects are flying?

Answer on page 290.

Monkey Business

The theater shows a double feature. The second movie is about Tarzan going into the moving business.

For his first job, Tarzan must raise a 35-pound crate into his neighbor's tree house. To do this, he first attaches a pulley to a tree branch. He then passes a rope through the pulley and ties it to the crate. Just as he is about to lift the crate, he is called away to help a nearby elephant.

A passing chimp observes the situation and decides to help. The chimp also weighs 35 pounds. As the chimp pulls down on the rope what happens to the crate?

Answer on page 291.

The Strangest Eyes

The scientist has transformed herself into a fly. One of her eyes is made up of one loop coiled into a spiral-like design. The other eye is made up of two separate loops shaped into a similar design. Can you tell which eye is the single loop and which one is the double without tracing the lines with a pencil?

Answer on page 291.

Now Seating?

Suppose two boys and three girls go to the movie theater and they all sit in the same row. If the row has only five seats:

1. How many different ways can the two boys and three girls be seated in this row?

2. What are the chances that the two children at the ends of the row are both boys?

3. What are the chances that the two children at the ends of the row are both girls?

Answer on page 290.

Möbius Strip

Here is one the strangest loops you'll ever see. It's called a Möbius strip in honor of the German mathematician who first investigated its properties.

To build a Möbius strip, you need a strip of paper about 1 inch wide and 10 inches long. Coil the paper into a simple loop. Then put a single twist in the loop before securing the ends together with a piece of tape. Use a marker to color one side of the strip red and the other side blue. You'll soon discover that this loop has only one side!

Möbius strips are used in manufacturing. Many machines have belts that are used to connect different spinning parts. By using a belt sewn into a Möbius strip, the belt wears evenly on both sides.

Suppose you divide right down the middle of the Möbius strip. What shape would you get? Make a guess; then use a pair of scissors to carefully divide the strip.

Answer on page 291.

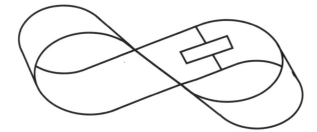

Head Count

In the final scene, a pet store owner is counting the birds and lizards that Tarzan has delivered to her store. For some odd reason, she decides to tally only the heads and scaly legs of these animals. When she has finished, she has counted thirty heads and seventy legs. How many birds and how many lizards are there?

Answer on page 291.

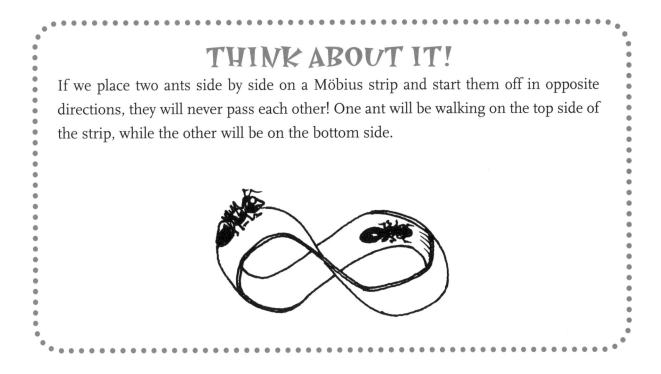
Squaring Off

Make a copy of these four rectangles. Cut out the shapes and then arrange them to form a perfect square.

Answer on page 291.

Ant Walk

Let's pick up an ant from the strip and place it on one corner of a sugar cube. This cube has sides all measuring 1 centimeter. If the ant can only walk along the edges of the cube, what is the total distance it can travel without retracing any part of its path?

Answer on page 291.

Cubic Quandaries

A wooden cube is painted red. Suppose it is divided with four equal cuts into the smaller cubes as shown.

1. How many smaller cubes are there?
2. How many of these smaller cubes
a. have only one side that is painted red?
b. have two sides that are painted red?
c. have three sides that are painted red?
d. have no sides that are red?

Answers on page 291.

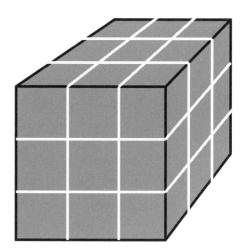

Saving Face

How good are you at visualizing things? These next few puzzles test your ability to rotate and construct objects in your mind.

These blocks below represent the same block. What figure is missing on the upper face of the last block?

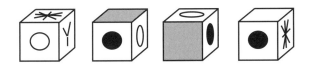

Which of the six cubes below can be created by folding this design?

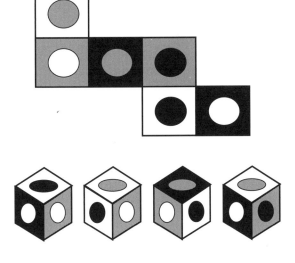

Finally, if you fold up this flat sheet along the inner lines, which figure represents the result?

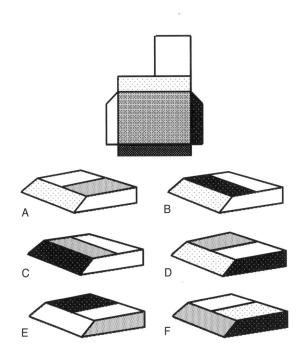

Answers on page 291.

Cut the Cards

Have you ever played cards and wished you had a different hand? Suppose you need a heart instead of a spade. Well, here's your chance to change one suit into another.

Photocopy the spade below. Then use a pair of scissors to cut it into three pieces so that the pieces can be fitted together to form a heart. Can you do it?

Answer on page 292.

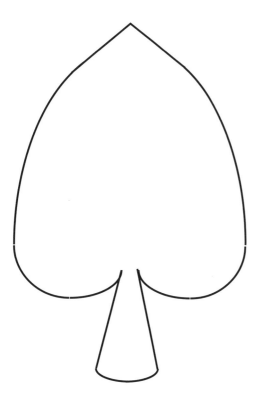

Stripped Stripe

There is a legend about a king who had six brothers and six sisters. His country's flag reflected this family structure with twelve bold stripes. When two of his brothers moved out of the kingdom, the king had two of the stripes removed.

Can you figure out how to cut the flag into as few pieces as possible so that the pieces can be put back together to make the same type of flag, but with two less stripes? No part of the flag can be discarded.

Answer on page 292.

Missing Square

Count the number of blocks that make up this pattern. If you don't want to count each block, you can multiply the number of rows by the number of columns to get a total of sixty-four blocks.

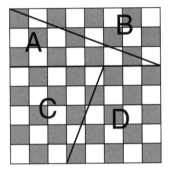

Now photocopy the pattern.

Using a pair of scissors, separate the checkerboard along the inner lines. Reassemble the pieces as shown below.

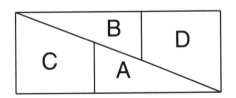

Now count the blocks, or, if you'd rather, just multiply again. The new figure is thirteen blocks long and five blocks high. That gives us sixty-five blocks. Where did the extra block come from?

Answer on page 292.

Tipping the Scales

What whole animal(s) must be added to balance the fourth scale?

Answer on page 292.

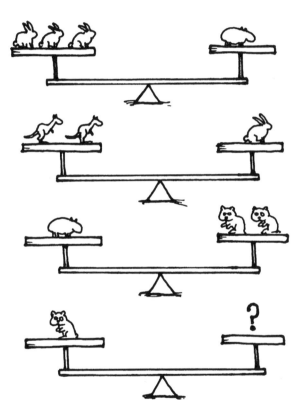

Snake Spread

These hungry snakes are swallowing each other. Since they began this odd dining experience, the circle they formed has gotten smaller. If they continue to swallow each other, what will eventually happen to the circle of snakes?

Answer on page 292.

Falcon Flight

Two bicyclists are situated 60 miles apart. One has a falcon on his shoulder. The bicyclists start riding toward each other at the same time, both maintaining a constant speed of 30 mph. The moment they begin, the falcon flies off the first cyclist's shoulder and towards the other. The falcon flies at a constant ground speed of 45 mph. When the falcon meets the other rider, he reverses direction and flies back to the first cyclist (who is now considerably closer). The falcon continues this back and forth pattern until the riders finally meet. How far did the falcon fly?

Answer on page 292.

A Question of Balance

Place two fingers at the ends of a yardstick. Slowly move the fingers toward each other. As you'll discover, your fingers always meet in the middle of the yardstick.

Now place both fingers in the middle of the stick. Slowly try moving the two of them out to the opposite ends. This time you'll find that one finger remains in the middle while the other moves to the end. Can you explain this behavior?

Answer on page 292.

Well-Balanced Plate

Here's a game that you are guaranteed to win as long as you let your opponent go first. Start with a plate on the exact center of a table. Your opponent must place another plate on the table. Then, it's your turn. During each turn, both of you must continue placing plates until no more plates will fit, but, don't worry, you'll win. Can you figure out the secret?

Answer on page 293.

Robot Walkers

Have you ever seen a robot walker? It is designed to move over various types of terrain so that scientists can use it to explore nearby planets. Our robot walkers are positioned at the corners of a square plot of land. Each robot is programmed to follow the robot directly ahead of it. If all the robots move at the same speed, what will happen to the square pattern? Will the robots ever meet?

Answer on page 293.

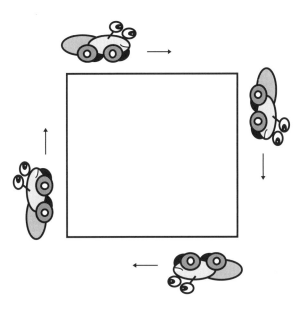

Chain Links

Suppose you own four pieces of chain. One chain has 5 links, two chains have 4 links, and one chain has 3 links.

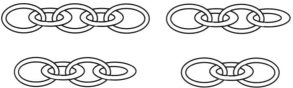

You go to the jeweler and ask her to make a bracelet using all of these chains. She says it would cost $.50 to break a link and $1.00 to weld a link together. You calculate that it would cost $6.00 to build the bracelet. The jeweler, however, says that it would only cost $4.50. Can figure out how she can assemble your bracelet for less?

Answer on page 293.

Money Magic

Look at the picture to your right. Can you guess what will happen when the bill is pulled from both ends?

After you've made your prediction, use a dollar bill and two paper clips to assemble this puzzle. Make sure that each paper clip grips only two of the three side-by-side sections. Slowly pull the bill apart. What happens to the clips? How is it possible?

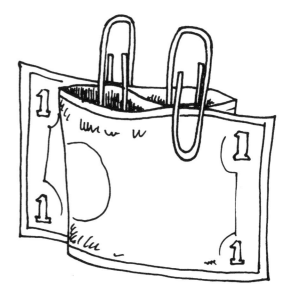

Answer on page 293.

Revolutionary Thoughts

Different things orbit the earth at various speeds and distances. For example, satellites and space instruments released by the space shuttle are only several hundred miles away from the earth, while communication satellites circle at a distance of about 22,300 miles!

In this puzzle, Satellite X-1 orbits our planet once every 9 hours, Satellite Beta once every $4^{1}/_{2}$ hours, and Satellite Parking once every 3 hours.

At time zero, the satellites are positioned in a straight line. How long will it take for all three objects to position themselves again in a straight line?

Answer on page 293.

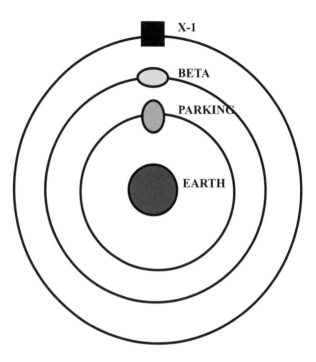

Rope Ruse

There is an old legend about an ancient magician who could tie a rope into a knot while holding on to each end of the rope. Can you?

Answer on page 293.

Baffling Holes

Black holes are celestial objects created by collapsed stars. These holes have tremendous concentration of matter and produce such a strong gravitational field that even light can't escape from it. If a black hole was placed on the surface of the earth, our entire planet would be sucked into it!

The hole in this puzzle is not as large as a black hole, but finding its solution can be a big challenge. Do you think a quarter can pass through a hole that is the size of a nickel? You can't tear, cut, or rip the hole. Impossible, you say? Trace the outline of a nickel onto an index card. Carefully cut out this outline.

HINT: Bends and twists can open up a whole new geometry.

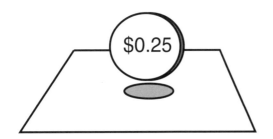

Solution on page 294.

A Giant Step

Passing a quarter through a nickel-sized hole is nothing when you can step through an index card. Carefully use a pair of scissors or a modeling knife to cut out the pattern of slots shown here. When you are finished, the hole will open in an accordion-like style and allow you to step through it!

A Fair Solution

Two teenagers are deciding how to share the last piece of pizza. One of them must divide the slice. Both are afraid that the other will cut the slice unfairly and take the larger piece. Can this conflict be resolved by these teenagers so that both will be satisfied by the other one's cut?

After finishing their pizza, the happy teenagers bring out a box of toothpicks and arrange the toothpicks as follows:
Can you remove four toothpicks and leave ten on the table?

Answers on pages 294.

Nuts!

When you rotate a bolt clockwise, it travels into the threads of a nut. When that same bolt is rotated counterclockwise, the nut and bolt will separate.

Suppose you have two bolts aligned within each other's threads. If both bolts are rotated clockwise, will they move together, separate, or remain the same distance apart?

Here's something else to think about. In many large cities, the light bulbs used in places such as subway stations are unique. Instead of screwing into the socket with a clockwise motion, they require counterclockwise turns. What sense does it make to have these different from most other bulbs?

Answers on page 294.

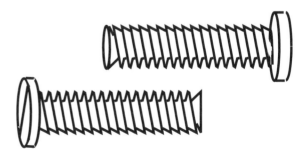

Sock It to Me

Did you know that a sock-like garment was first worn by Greek women? This soft leather covering appeared around 600 B.C. and was called a "sykhos." Roman women copied the style and changed the name to "soccus."

Let's open your "soccus" drawer. Suppose you have four pairs of black socks, three pairs of white socks, and a pair of red socks. It is nighttime and you can't see the colors of the socks. You need to select one pair of matching socks. Any color will do.

What is the least number of socks you need to remove from the draw to insure that you have at least one matching pair?

Answer on page 294.

Doubtful Dimensions

John wants to ship a baseball bat to his sister. The bat is 4 feet, 11 inches long. He places it in a rectangular box that is 5 feet long. When he takes it to the shipper, they can't send the package because it is too long. All dimensions of the package must be 4 feet or less in order to be shipped.

When John returns home, he figures out how he can repack the bat. What does he do?

Answer on page 294.

Machine Madness

The identical wheels of this machine are connected by a series of belts. The outer rim of each wheel has a circumference of 8 centimeters. The rim of each wheel's inner shaft has a circumference of 4 centimeters. If the crank is rotated up one-quarter turn, what hour would the clock's hand point to?

Answer on page 294.

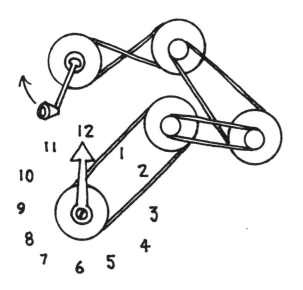

Putting It Together

Suppose you have a list of numbers from one to one hundred. How quickly can you add them all up without using a calculator?

HINT: There is a swift way to add these numbers. Think about how the numbers at the opposite ends of the list relate to each other.

Answer on page 294.

The Heat Is On

The next time you drive under a highway bridge, take a close look at its ends. It is most likely that one end of the bridge will be attached directly to the road. The other end, however, will probably have a small gap. The gap is there on purpose. When the temperature rises, the bridge expands. If the gap wasn't there, the expanding metal bridge might shatter the roadway!

How about holes? Do they also expand when heated? Suppose a metal washer is placed in a flame. What happens to the size of its hole?

Answer on page 294.

City Pipes

Beneath almost every city is an intricate system of large water-carrying pipes. These pipes transport runoff that falls through sewer openings and keep the city streets from flooding when there's a rainstorm.

The pipes are connected to the surface through manhole openings. Manhole covers fit over the openings. How does their shape prevent them from falling into the hole?

HINT: Think of how the bat from the "Doubtful Dimensions" puzzle on page 158 was packaged!

Answer on page 294.

Magic Square

Take a look at the grid below. Like the "Magic Pyramid" puzzle presented on page 9 of this book, the Magic Square is created when the right numbers are placed in the empty boxes.

Place a number from 1 to 9 in each of the boxes below. Don't repeat any of the numbers. Their arrangement must result in any row of three numbers (vertical, horizontal, or diagonal) adding to 15.

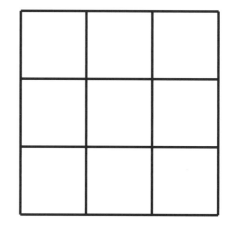

Answer on page 295.

Anti-Magic Square

Like the Magic Square, the Anti-Magic Square uses the same grid as above, except you have to place the numbers 1 to 9 to create a square where each row's sum is different.

Think that's easy? Give it a try. Remember, you can't repeat any of the numbers.

Answer on page 295.

What's Next?

Take a look at the pattern below. These symbols have a logical order. Can you draw the next symbol in the sequence?

HINT: A little reflection with your thinking skills may help you solve this puzzle.

Answer on page 295.

Numbers Game

Here's another game that you're bound to win as long as you let your opponent go first.

The object of the game is simple. The first one to reach 100 wins!

Each round involves adding a number from 1 to 10 to the previous number. Your opponent goes first and identifies a number from 1 to 10. You add to that number and announce the sum. The turns continue until 100 is reached.

The winning strategy is for you to always produce the key numbers, which are 12, 23, 34, 45, 56, 67, 78, 89, and the winning 100.

So if your opponent says 8, you add 4 and get to the first key number 12. You continue adding to the keys, and within nine rounds you'll be a winner.

Now suppose you can only add a number from 1 to 5 to your opponent's number until you reach 50.

What would the key numbers now be?

Answer on page 295.

Another Ant Walk

A queen ant finds herself climbing onto the metal framework of a bridge at the spot marked by the arrow.

Can you trace the path she'd need to follow in order to walk across every piece of frame only once and end up at the top of the bridge (marked by an X)?

Her path must be a continuous line.

Answer on page 295.

In Order

Examine the set of pictures on the next page. Can you place them in their most logical order?

Answer on page 295.

Connect the Dots

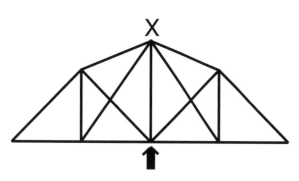

Starting at the top center dot, can you connect all of the other nine dots with only four straight lines? The four lines must all be connected and your pencil can't leave the paper while drawing the answer.

Answer on page 295.

Tangrams

In Asia, tangrams are known as "the seven plates of wisdom." No wonder, since this Chinese puzzle, probably one of the most famous dissection games, has been around for at least several hundred years.

A tangram consists of five triangles, a square, and a rhomboid.

To get these shapes, copy the lines shown below onto a square sheet of heavy stock paper. Use a pair of scissors to cut out each of the seven sections.

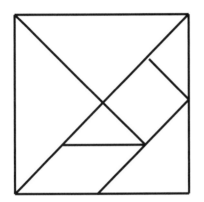

Another way you can make the seven shapes is to start with a square sheet of paper.

2. Cut one of the triangles in half to make two equal triangles (Sections I and II).

3. Fold back the corner of the other triangle and cut along this fold to get another triangle (Section III).

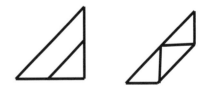

4. Cut the remaining piece into two equal halves.

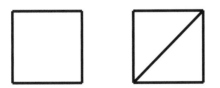

1. Cut the square in half to make two large triangles.

5. Fold and cut one of the pieces to get a square and right triangle. (Sections IV and V).

6. Fold and cut the other piece like this (Sections VI and VII).

With your seven pieces, try and create these figures.

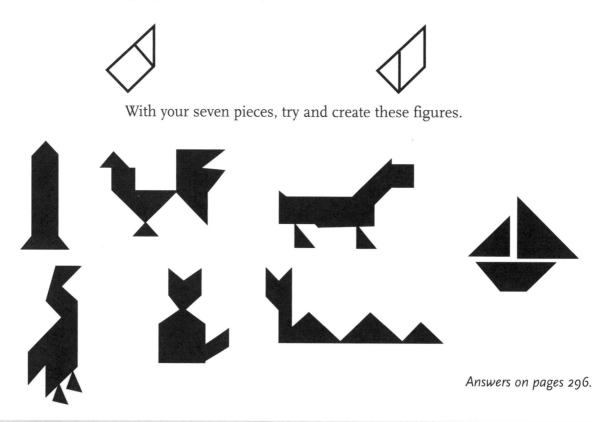

Answers on pages 296.

Fractured Farmland

While flying over farmland, a pilot notices the rectangular shape of the fields below. She sketches the lines that divide the fields.

When she returns to the airport, she wonders how many different rectangles can be formed by the lines drawn below?

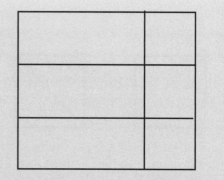

HINT: Don't forget that a square is also a rectangle.

Answer on page 296.

Number Sense

The number symbols we use are called Arabic numerals. Logically, they originated in the Middle East. Right? Wrong. They were created in India. Europeans learned these symbols from Arabic scholars and, inadvertently, the name Arabic numeral stuck.

Now try not to get stuck on this number problem. Can you uncover the logic used to place each of the numbers below? If so, what number should be placed at the question mark?

Answer on page 296.

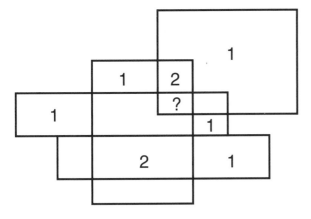

What Comes Next?

In the next page, choose the next logical member of the sequence.

Answer on page 296.

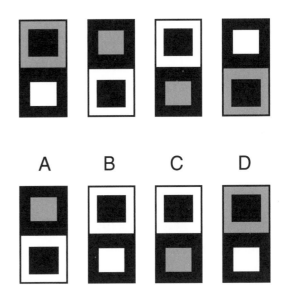

The Marked Park

Jethro's custom racer has two different-sized tires. The smaller front tire has a circumference of 7 feet. The larger rear tire has a circumference of 9 feet.

Rita, the meter maid, sees Jethro's racer parked in a 10-minute zone and decides to mark the curbside tires with a spot of paint. She places a mark on the front and rear tires exactly where each tire touches the ground.

Twenty minutes later, Rita returns. She sees both marks still touching the ground. As she begins writing a parking ticket, Jethro returns and explains that he did move his racer. In fact, he moved it the exact distance required to rotate the marks back into their same relative position. Assuming Jethro is telling the truth, what is the shortest distance that the racer was moved?

Answer on page 296.

Pattern Path

All of the numbers below form a sequence. Can you figure out the logic of the sequence? If so, begin at the point marked start and trace a path from box to box. The boxes can be connected horizontally, vertically, or diagonally. Double and triple digit numbers can be made by grouping the numbers this way. You can go through a box only once. Your mission is to finish at the stop sign located in the bottom right corner.

Answer on page 297.

Start

2	1	6	4	2	4
8	4	3	2	0	8
6	2	6	1	0	4
1	4	5	5	2	0
2	8	2	1	9	6

Stop

Pile Puzzler

Cards can be arranged in many different orders. Don't try all of them unless you have time to count 80,660,000, 000,000,000,000,000,000,000,000,00 0,000,000,000,000,000,000,000,000, 000,000,000

Here's a card challenge that has fewer solutions. Exchange one card from each of the piles to form three piles with equal sums.

In this puzzle, the Ace only counts as one. Only one card can be exchanged from each pile.

Answer on page 297.

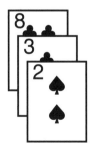 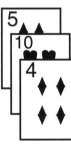 

Pattern Puzzler

The five numbers within each circle represent a mathematical relationship. This same relationship is displayed in each of the four circles.

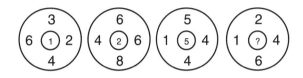

Using this pattern, what is the most likely value for the question mark in the last circle?

Answer on page 297.

Titillating Tiles

There's a tile below that doesn't fit with the other four in the group.

Can you figure out the relationship of the tiles and find the one that is different?

Answer on page 297.

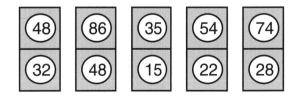

Pattern Grid

A pattern grid is filled with items based on a geometric arrangement to form a visual pattern. Examine the grid below for a pattern and then try to select the section that completes it.

Answer on page 297.

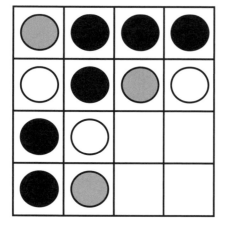

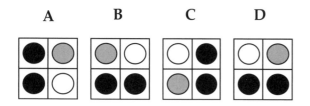

Brain Net

Your brain is an incredible piece of machinery. About the size of a squished softball, it contains billions of brain cells. These cells make more connections than all of the phones in the world. It's this huge network that produces your brain power! Want to feel the "brain net" in action?

Take a look at the drawing below. Your job is to figure out how many different paths can get you across from start to finish.

You can only move to the right. You can't go back. When you arrive at a "fork," take either the top or bottom route. Start counting.

Answer on page 297.

Predicting Paths

One of your brain's most powerful capabilities is the ability to think visually. When we think in this way, we construct a mind's eye image of a shape, scene, or concept. This image can be rotated, changed, moved, and analyzed. How good are you at visual thinking? Here's your first chance to find out.

Suppose we roll the wheel along the flat surface. Draw the shape that would be traced by the point within the wheel.

Now let's put the small wheel along the inner rim of a larger circle. What shape path would a point on the smaller wheel trace?

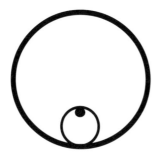

Finally, suppose the inner wheel remains stationary. What pattern would be traced out by a point on the larger rim as it rolls around (and remains in contact with) the inner wheel?

Answers on pages 297.

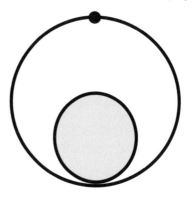

Who's That?

Look into a mirror and who do you see? You? Perhaps, but it's not the same you that everyone else sees. Its a right-left reversed image. The ear that appears on your left side is seen by others on your right side.

Suppose you want to see yourself exactly as others see you. How can you set up two small mirrors so that your reflection isn't reversed?

Answer on page 297.

Leftovers Again?

Your brain is divided into two halves. The left half is more number-oriented, rational, and concrete. Your right half is more creative, playful, and artistic. To solve this next puzzle, you'll have to borrow a little from both sides of your brain.

In an art class, students are taught how to shape a 1 ounce bag of clay into a small statue. During this process, some clay remains unused (actually, it falls to the floor). For every five statues that are made, there is enough extra clay to make one more statue. Suppose a student is presented with 25 ounces of clay. What is the maximum number of statues he can sculpt?

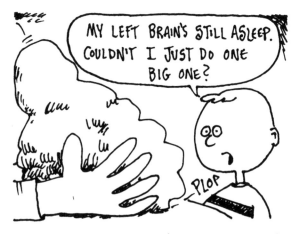

Answer on pages 298.

Brownie Cut

Now that art class is over, it's time for cooking class.

A chocolate brownie emerges from the oven. Karen cuts the square brownie in half. She then divides one of the halves into two smaller but equal parts.

Before she can eat the larger piece, two of her friends unexpectedly arrive. Karen wants everyone to have the same amount of dessert. In the fewest number of cuts, how can she produce three equal portions?

Answer on page 298.

Balancing Gold

A gold bar balances with nine-tenths of 1 pound and nine-tenths of a similar gold bar. How much does each gold bar weigh?

Answer on page 298.

Tricky Tide

In the Bay of Fundy, the tides can vary in height by almost 50 feet. The bay in our puzzle has a tidal range of only 6 feet. A boat moors in the middle of this bay. A ladder hangs down from the deck of the boat and touches the flat sea surface. The rungs are 1 foot apart.

At low tide, ten rungs of the ladder are exposed. At high tide, the water level rises 6 feet. How many of the rungs will remain exposed?

Answer on page 298.

Thrifty Technique

Don't put that balance away! You'll need it along with a few pounds of brain cells to help solve this next problem.

By the way, did you know that Albert Einstein's brain was "normal" in weight? For the most part, it resembled an ordinary brain. There was, however, a slight difference. He had extra "cleanup" cells (called neuroglial cells). These cells move around the brain to get rid of dead or injured nerve cells. Perhaps his "well swept" brain supercharged his intelligence?

You have nine gold coins. One of the coins is counterfeit and is filled with a lighter-than-gold substance. Using a balance, what strategy can you use to uncover the counterfeit coin?

To make things a little more difficult, you must identify the fake coin with only two uses of the balance.

Answer on pages 298.

Breaking Up Is Hard to Do

How fast can you think? Faster than a speeding bullet? Faster than electricity? For most of us, thoughts race around our brains between 3 to 300 mph. Who knows, this puzzle may break your brain's speed record.

The square encloses a 4 x 4 grid. There are five different ways this grid can be divided into identical quarters. Each way uses a different shape. Can you uncover the layout of all five patterns?

Answer on page 298.

Disorder

Buildings crumble. Living things decompose. It's a scientific principle that things tend to go from order to disorder. The fancy name for this principle is entropy. There are, however, a few things that appear to go against this tendency. Crystals grow and become more complex. Living things take simple chemicals and build complex tissues.

This puzzle, however, uses entropy. Notice how neat and orderly the arrangement of numbers is. Now, let's play the entropy game and rearrange the numbers so that no two consecutive numbers touch each other. They cannot align side by side, up and down, or diagonally.

Answer on page 298.

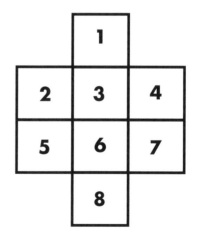

True or False?

Here's a totally different type of problem. This one is based on logic.

Two cultures of aliens live on the planet Trekia, the carpals and the tarsals. The carpals always lie. The tarsals always tell the truth.

A space traveler arrives on Trekia and meets a party of three aliens. She asks the aliens to which culture they belong. The first one murmurs something that is too soft to hear. The second replies, "It said it was a carpal." The third says to the second, "You are a liar!" From this information, figure out what culture the third alien belongs to.

Answer on page 299.

Pack Up Your Troubles

A fragile item is to be shipped in a cardboard box. In order to prevent the item from hitting against the walls of the box, plastic foam cubes are used as "bumpers." There are ten of these cubes. How can you position them along the inner walls of the box so that there is an equal number of cubes along each wall?

Answer on page 299.

Don't Come Back This Way Again!

The pitcher plant is a carnivorous plant that eats insects. An unfortunate insect walks into the pitcher plant's flower. When it tries to reverse direction, it can't. Tiny spines on the petals' surface face downward, which forces the insect to move in one direction—down.

Here's your chance not to go back. The shape below is made with one continuous line. Starting anywhere, can you complete the shape without lifting your pencil from the page? As you probably guessed, your path cannot cross over itself.

Answer on page 299.

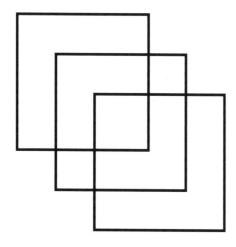

Meet Me on the Edge

Did you know that an ant can lift about fifty times its body weight? If you had that power, you'd be able to lift over 2 tons! Suppose we position one of those powerful ants on a corner of a sugar cube. On the opposite corner, we position a fly. Suppose the two insects begin walking towards each other. If they can only walk along the edges of the cube (and never go backwards), what is the probability that their paths will cross?

Answer on page 299.

Only the Shadow Knows?

A medium-size jet has a wingspan of 120 feet. An albatross is a bird with a wingspan of about 12 feet. At what altitude would each object have to fly in order to cast shadows of equal size?

Answer on page 299.

More Shadow Stuff

At a certain time of day, a 25-foot telephone pole casts a 10-foot shadow. At that same time, how high would a tree have to be in order to cast a 25-foot shadow?

Answer on page 299.

Trip Times

Did you know that the speed record for cars is over 700 miles per hour? To attain this supersonic speed, the cars use rocket engines. They move so quickly that if the car body had wings, the vehicle would fly! The car in our problem is much slower. In 1 hour, traveling at 30 mph, it climbs to the top of the hill. When the car reaches the top, the driver remembers that she left her field guide to mountain life back home. She immediately turns around and drives downhill at 60 mph. Assuming that she spent no time at the top, what was her average speed?

HINT: It is not 45 mph.

Answer on page 299.

Average Puzzle

How fast can you ride a bicycle? To get into the Guinness Book of Records for human-powered cycling, you'd need to ride faster than 60 mph.

An ordinary cyclist travels up and down a hill. Going up, she maintains a constant speed of 10 mph. It takes her 1 hour to get to the top. Assuming that the hill is symmetric, what speed must she maintain on the way going down if she wishes to average 20 mph? Before you bask in victory, the answer is not 30 mph.

Answer on page 300.

Palindrome

A palindrome is a word or number that reads the same backwards as it does forward. Numbers such as 606 and 4334 are palindromes.

While driving his car, Bob (so much of a palindrome lover that he changed his name from John to Bob) observes that the odometer reading forms a palindrome. It displays the mileage 13,931.

Bob keeps driving. Two hours later, he looks at the odometer again and, to his surprise, it displays a different palindrome!

What is the most likely speed that Bob is traveling?

Answer on page 300.

Stacking Up

Can you arrange these numbered blocks into three equal stacks so that the sum of the numbers displayed in each stack must be equal to any other stack.

Answer on page 300.

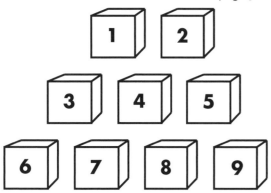

Crossing Hands

Picture in your mind a clock with a face and hands. Between the hours of 5 am and 5 pm, how many times will the hour and minute hands cross each other?

Answer on page 300.

Star Birth

Trace this octagon pattern onto a separate sheet of paper. Then decide how to divide this shape into eight identical triangles that can be arranged into a star. The star will have eight points and an octagon-shaped hole in its center. When you think you've come up with an answer, trace the pattern onto the octagon. Cut out the separate parts and reassemble them into a star.

Answer on page 300.

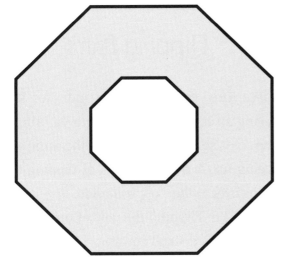

Flip Flop

Did you know that the ancient Egyptians believed that triangles had sacred qualities? This may have led to the superstition about walking under a ladder. When a ladder is placed against a wall, it forms a triangle. To walk through the triangle might provoke the wrath of the gods.

The triangle below is made up of ten disks. Can you move three of the disks to make the triangle point in the opposite direction?

Answer on page 300.

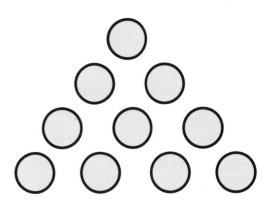

177

What's Next?

Examine the figures below. Can you see what the pattern is and find out what the fourth figure in this series should look like?

Answer on page 301.

Trying Triangles

How many triangles can be found in this figure?

Answer on page 301.

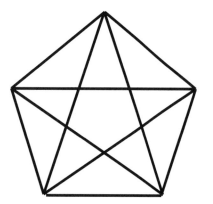

Flipping Pairs

Place three coins with their indicated side facing up as shown. In three moves, arrange the coins so that all three have the same side facing up. A move consists of flipping two coins over to their opposite side.

NOTE: Flipping the pair of outer coins three times doesn't count!

Answer on page 301.

Missing Blocks

Examine the figure of blocks below. Let's assume that the hidden blocks are all in place. How many additional blocks are needed to fill in the empty region to complete this cube?

Once you've made your guess, look at the pattern again. Assume that the hidden blocks are all in place. Now let's suppose that all of the blocks you can see are vaporized. How many blocks would be left behind?

Answers on page 301.

Matchstick Memories

Years ago, matchsticks were made from small sections of wood. These common and inexpensive objects were perfect props for after-dinner or parlor room activities. Nowadays, toothpicks offer the same advantages. So get your picks together and arrange them in the three patterns shown below.

As you can see, each line of matchsticks forms an incorrect equation. The challenge is to make each one correct by changing the position of only one of the toothpicks in each row.

Answers on page 301.

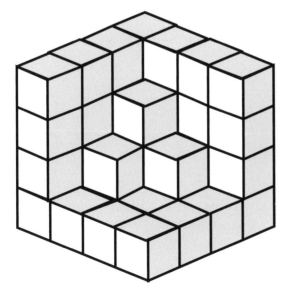

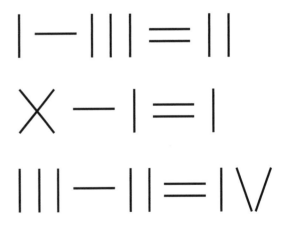

Sum Circle

Place the numbers one through six within the six smaller circles shown below. Each number must be used only once. The numbers must be placed so that the sum of the four numbers that fall on a circle's circumference is equal to the sum of the numbers on any other circle's circumference.

Think it's easy? Give it a try.

Answer on page 301.

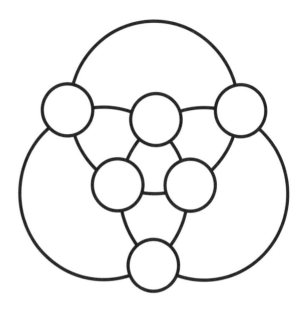

- -

Many Rivers to Cross

Let's take a break from puzzles and go on a rowboat ride across the river. There are four adults who want to cross it. They come upon a boy and a girl playing in a rowboat. The boat can hold either two children or one adult. Can the adults succeed in crossing the river? If so, how?

Answer on page 301.

Train Travel

A train travels at a constant rate of speed. It reaches a stretch of track that has fifteen poles. The poles are placed at an equal distance to each other. It takes the train 10 minutes to travel from the first pole to the tenth pole. How long will it take the train to reach the fifteenth pole?

Answer on page 301-302.

PLEASE, HOLMES. CAN WE GO HOME IF YOU DON'T FIGURE IT OUT THIS TRIP?

Miles Apart

The distance from New York to Boston is 220 miles. Suppose a train leaves Boston for New York and travels at 65 mph. One hour later, a train leaves New York for Boston and travels at 55 mph. If we assume the tracks are straight paths and the trains maintain a constant speed, how far apart are the trains 1 hour before they meet?

Answer on page 302.

Passing Trains

Coming from opposite directions, a freight train and a passenger train pass each other on parallel tracks. The passenger train travels at 60 mph. The freight train travels at 30 mph. A passenger observes that it takes 6 seconds to pass the freight train. How many feet long is the freight train?

HINT: There are 5,280 feet in a mile.

Answer on page 302.

Souped-Up Survey

A survey agency reported their results in the local newspaper. The report states that exactly one hundred local lawyers were interviewed. Of the one hundred, seventy-five lawyers own BMWs, ninety-five lawyers own Volvos, and fifty lawyers own both a BMW and a Volvo. Within a short time after the report, several lawyers argue that the survey results are incorrect. How can they tell?

Answer on page 302.

Toasty

In order to make French toast, Ricardo must fry both sides of a bread slice for 30 seconds. His frying pan can only hold two slices of bread at once. How can he make three slices of French toast in only 1½ minutes instead of 2 minutes?

Answer on page 302.

Circle Game

Examine the pattern of circles below. Can you place the numbers one through nine in these circles so that the sum of the three circles connected vertically, horizontally, or diagonally is equal to fifteen?

Answer on page 302.

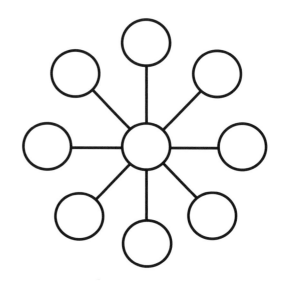

A Fare Split

Michelle rents a car to take her to the airport in the morning and return her home that evening. Halfway to the airport, she picks up a friend who accompanies her to the airport. That night, she and her friend return back to Michelle's home. The total cost is $20.00. If the amount to be paid is to be split fairly, how much money should Michelle pay?

Answer on page 303.

Pentagon Parts

The pentagon below is divided into five equal parts. Suppose you color one or more parts gray. How many different and distinguishable patterns can you form? Each pattern must be unique and not be duplicated by simply rotating the pentagon.

Answer on page 303.

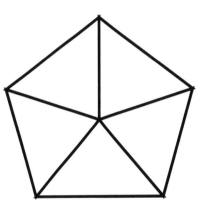

Bagel for Five?

You and four friends have decided to split a bagel for breakfast. The five of you are not fussy about the size of the piece each will receive. In other words, all the pieces don't have to be the same size.

Using two perfectly straight cuts, is it possible to divide this bagel into five pieces?

Answer on page 303.

Coin Moves

Place twelve coins in the pattern shown below. Notice how they form the corners of six equal-sized squares. Can you remove three of the coins to have only three equal-sized squares remaining?

Answer on page 303.

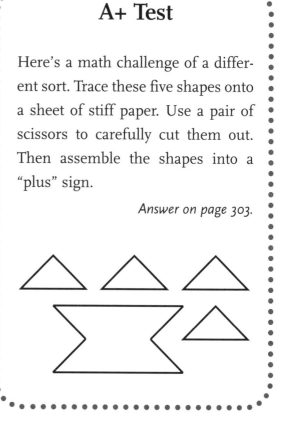

Trapezoid Trap

Divide the trapezoid below into four identical parts.

Answer on page 303.

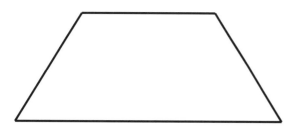

A+ Test

Here's a math challenge of a different sort. Trace these five shapes onto a sheet of stiff paper. Use a pair of scissors to carefully cut them out. Then assemble the shapes into a "plus" sign.

Answer on page 303.

Measuring Mug

Without the aid of any measuring device, how can you use a transparent 16-ounce mug to measure a volume of water that is exactly 8 ounces?

Answer on pages 303-304.

Coin Roll

Two identical coins are positioned side by side. In your mind's eye, roll the coin on the left (Coin A) over the other coin (Coin B). When Coin A reaches the opposite side of Coin B, stop. In which direction will Coin A's head be facing?

Now, let's suppose that Coin A rolls completely around Coin B. If so, how many rotations does Coin A make around its own center?

Answers on page 304.

Mis-Marked Music

There are three boxes filled with audiocassette tapes. One box contains rap tapes, another contains jazz tapes, while the third contains both rap and jazz tapes. All three boxes have labels identifying the type of tapes within. The only problem is that all of the boxes are mislabeled.

By selecting only one box and listening to only one tape, how can you label all three boxes correctly?

Answer on page 303.

Magic Triangle

Here's a magic triangle whose sides are formed by sets of four numbers. To solve the puzzle, place the numbers one through nine each in one of the circles. When you are finished, the sums of all three sides must be equal.

There are three different sums that can be used to reach the solution. Can you find all three?

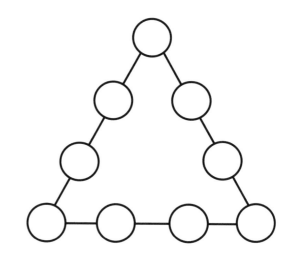

Answers on page 304.

Patterns

The arrangement of numbers below represents a pattern. This pattern is a mathematical relationship between the numbers in each square, so don't look for things like spelling, days of the week, cryptograms, or codes. Can you uncover the pattern and fill in the question mark in the last square?

Answer on page 304.

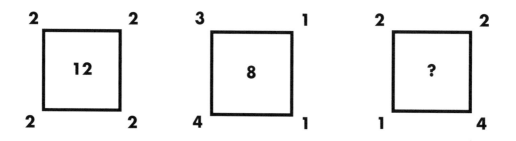

Painting on the Side

You are presented with several white cubes and a bucket of red paint. To make each of them different, you decide to paint one or more sides of each cube red. How many distinguishable cubes can you make with this painting method? Remember that any painted side must be painted completely to make it distinguishable from any other painted side.

Answer on page 304.

Frog Jump

A frog falls into a well that is 18 feet deep. Every day the frog jumps up a total distance of 6 feet. At night, as the frog grips the slimy well walls, it slips back down by 2 feet. At this rate, how many days will it take the frog to jump to the rim of the well?

Answer on page 304.

Army Ants

Two small armies of ants meet head-on along a jungle path. Both armies would prefer to pass each other rather than fight. There is a small space along the side of the path. It is only large enough to hold one ant at a time. Is it possible for the armies to pass each other? If so, how?

Answer on page 305.

No Sweat

There are six players on a coed volley-ball team. After an exhausting game, each girl drinks 4 cups of water. Each boy drinks 7 cups of water. The coach drinks 9 cups.

A total of 43 cups of water is consumed by everyone. How many boys and how many girls are on the team?

Answer on page 305.

Go Figure!

In a distant planet, there are four forms of life beings: zadohs, pugwigs, kahoots, and zingzags. All zadohs are pugwigs. Some pugwigs are kahoots. All kahoots are zingzags.

Which of the following statement(s) must then be true?

1. Some zadohs are zingzags.
2. Some kahoots are zadohs.
3. All kahoots are pugwigs.
4. Some zingzags are pugwigs.
5. All zingzags are zadohs.
6. Some zadohs are kahoots.

Answer on page 305.

Square Pattern

Suppose you have to paint all nine squares in the grid below using one of three colors: red, blue, or green. How many different patterns can you paint if each color must be represented in every row and every column? Each pattern must be unique. In other words, a new pattern can't be made by simply rotating the grid.

Answer on page 305.

Bouncing Ball

Did you know that when a ball strikes the ground, its shape distorts? This distortion stores the energy that powers its rebound. The more its shape changes, the higher the ball will bounce.

The ball in this puzzle rebounds to half the height from which it is dropped. Suppose it is dropped from a 1 meter height. What distance would the ball travel before it comes to rest?

Answer on pages 305.

Complete the Pattern

Use the pattern below to determine the value for X and Y.

Answer on page 305.

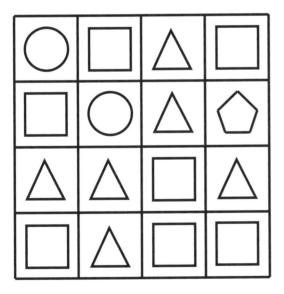

Checkerboard

A full-size checkerboard has eight rows and eight columns that make up its sixty-four squares. By combining the patterns of these squares, you can put together another 140 squares. The pattern below is one-fourth the area of a full size checkerboard. What is the total number of squares that are found in this smaller pattern?

Answer on page 305.

Cutting Edge

Kristin wants to remodel her home. To save money, she decides to move a carpet from one hallway to another. The carpet currently fills a passage that is 3 x 12 feet. She wishes to cut the carpet into two sections that can be joined together to fit a long and narrow hallway that is 2 x 18 feet. What does her cut look like?

Answer on page 306.

The Die Is Cast

Which die is unlike the other three?

Answer on pages 306.

Another Pattern

Here is another mathematical pattern that relates the four numbers of each triangle. Can you uncover the pattern and use it to complete the third triangle?

Answer on page 306.

4   5   2   10

5   5   5   5

4   1   1   ?

Playing with Matches?

Thirty-two soccer teams enter a statewide competition. The teams are paired randomly in each round. The winning team advances to the next round. Losers are eliminated. How many matches must be played in order to crown one winner?

Answer on page 306.

Competing Clicks

Let the Mouse Click Competition Begin! Emily can click a mouse ten times in 10 seconds. Buzzy can click a mouse twenty times in 20 seconds. Anthony can click a mouse five times in 5 seconds. Assume that the timing period begins with the first mouse click and ends with the final click. Which one of these computer users would be the first to complete forty clicks?

Answer on page 306.

Pizza Cut

Five people want to share a square pizza. The first person (who is really hungry) removes a quarter of the pie. When the others find out, they are annoyed and try to divide the remaining three-fourths into four equal and identically shaped slices. The cuts must be straight. How must they cut the remaining pizza in order to produce four identical slices?

Answer on page 306.

Vive le Flag

The French tricolor flag is made up of three vertical stripes: red, white, and blue. Suppose you are given four different colors of fabric and asked to create a different flag using the same tricolor design. If no two adjacent stripes can be the same color, how many different combinations of color patterns are there?

HINT: Don't forget that the flag pattern can be flipped over!

Answer on page 306.

A, B, See?

Each letter stands for a different digit in each equation. Can you decode each one?

Answers on page 307.

```
   AB        AA       ABA        ABA
   AB       +AA      +BAB       +BAA
  ───       ───      ────       ────
  ABB       BBC      BBBC       CDDD
```

Slip Sliding

For this challenge, you'll need to get seven coins. Place a coin on any of the star's eight points. Then slide the coin along one of the straight lines to its endpoint. Place a second coin on another point. Slide this one down to its endpoint. Continue in this manner until all seven coins have been placed.

NOTE: It can be done—but you'll need to develop a strategy.

Answer on page 307.

Spare Change

Jonathan has a pocket full of coins. Yet he doesn't have the right combination of coins to make change for a nickel, dime, quarter, half dollar, or dollar.

What is the largest value of coins Jonathan can have in his pocket?

Answer on page 307.

Puzzling Prices

A puzzle book costs $5.00 plus one-half of its price. How much does the puzzle book cost?

HINT: It's more expensive than this book.

Answer on page 307.

Gum Drop

In preparation for a party, Heather fills a large jar with gum drops. Before the party begins, Michael sees the gum drop jar. He (hoping that no one will realize) takes one-third of the drops. Soon after, Tanya takes one-third of the gum drops (she too hopes that no one will notice). Finally, Britt appears and, like the others, she takes one-third of the gum drops. If forty gum drops are left in the jar, how many did it originally contain?

Answer on page 307.

I RECOMMEND YOU QUIT GOING TO HEATHER'S PARTIES.

Go-Cart Crossing

Three go-cart tracks are built as shown. Each track forms a separate one-third of a mile loop. Three go-carts begin riding at the same time from the central point where all three tracks cross. One go-cart travels at 6 mph, another at 12 mph, and the third at 15 mph. How long will it take for all three go-carts to cross paths for the fifth time?

Answer on page 307.

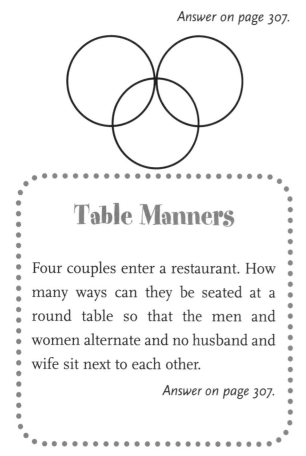

Table Manners

Four couples enter a restaurant. How many ways can they be seated at a round table so that the men and women alternate and no husband and wife sit next to each other.

Answer on page 307.

Winning Slip

A contest is fixed. Everyone knows it, including the contestants. One of the contestants, however, makes it to the final playoff level.

The master of ceremonies presents the following challenge: "This box contains two slips of paper. One slip has the word 'winner' printed on it, the other has the word 'loser.' Your task is to select the winning slip—without looking of course." The contestant knows that this challenge is fixed. He realizes that both slips have the word 'loser.' How can he select one slip and win the challenge? By the way, the contestant can't declare this contest is a fraud or he'd lose his current winnings.

Answer on page 307-308.

194

Ancient Man

An ancient Greek was said to have lived one-fourth of his life as a boy, one-fifth as a youth, one-third as a man, and spent the last 13 years as an elderly gent. How old was he when he died?

Answer on page 308.

Lights Out!

The total output of electrical energy from your brain is only about 20 watts. That's not an avalanche of power (especially when you consider that most household light bulbs use five times that amount). Now try powering up with this problem.

Imagine that you can't sleep because you are kept awake by the flashing neon lights that shine through a square store window. The window measures 10 x 10 feet.

A friend assures you that he can cover up half the area of the window but still leave a square section that is 10 x 10 feet. This will then satisfy both you and the storekeeper. You think your friend has lost it. Has he?

Answer on page 308.

Pencil Puzzle

Can you uncover the logic used to create this layout? If so, use that same logic to determine the letter for the question mark.

Answer on pages 308.

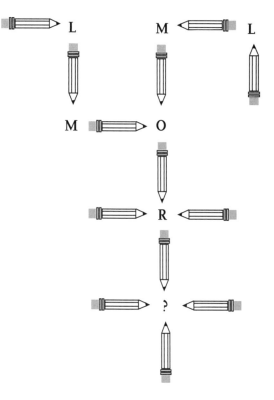

Sounds Logical?

It's the weekend! Saturdays and Sundays are the days that Sheila, Ramon, and Niko shop together for music. The CDs they purchase are either rock 'n' roll or jazz. When they visit the music store, each person will purchase one and only one CD. Here are the rules that govern their selections.

1. Either Sheila or Ramon will pick rock 'n' roll, but not both of them.
2. If Sheila picks rock 'n' roll, Niko picks jazz.
3. Niko and Ramon do not both pick jazz.

Which one of the three purchased a jazz CD on Saturday and a rock 'n' roll CD on Sunday?

Answer on page 308

Triangular Tower

Suppose ten billiard balls are placed in the standard triangular rack. If additional billiard balls are placed on top of this pattern, some balls will roll into the gullies to form a smaller, stable triangle (forget about the balls which roll off the stack). If you add more layers, you'll eventually build a billiard ball pyramid. How many billiard balls and levels would the pyramid contain?

Answer on page 308.

Criss-Crossed

Place six coins in the layout as shown below. Notice that this arrangement forms two columns. The horizontal column has four coins. The vertical column has three coins. Can you move only one coin to form two columns with each containing four coins?

Answer on page 308.

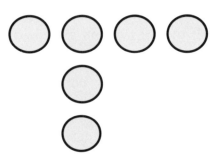

196

Crystal Building

Have you ever looked closely at a crystal? If so, you may have noticed that the crystal has flat sides and uniform angles. That's because a crystal is a repeating arrangement of tiny particles of matter. Often, a central particle is surrounded on all sides by other particles. Here's a puzzle that will help you visualize a crystal pattern.

Suppose you coat a tennis ball with glue. What is the maximum number of tennis balls that can attach directly to this sticky surface?

Answer on page 309.

Testy Target

Ten arrows are shot at the target below. One of them misses the target completely. The others all strike it. If the total sum of points is one hundred, in which part of the target did each arrow strike?

Answer on page 309.

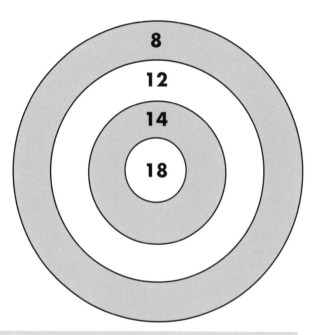

Planet Rotation

Our planet spins counterclockwise on its axis. It also has a counterclockwise revolution around the sun. Suppose both motions now go clockwise. How would this affect the apparent direction of sunrise and sunset?

Answer on page 309.

Eighth Century Enigma

Here's a puzzle that can be traced back to the eighth century. A man has a goat, a wolf, and a head of cabbage. He comes to a river and must bring these three things across to the other side. The boat can only take the man plus either the goat, wolf, or cabbage. There is another problem. If the cabbage is left with the goat, the goat will eat the cabbage. If the wolf is left with the goat, the goat will be devoured. How can he transport the wolf, goat, and cabbage to the other side?

Answer on page 309.

Shuffle

Pretend you have five cards: a ten, a jack, a queen, a king, and an ace. In your mind's eye, shuffle these five cards together and put the pile face down. If you were to select four cards, returning each card and reshuffling the deck after each pick, what kind of hand would you more likely draw: four Aces or a straight picked in sequence? Can you explain why?

Answer on page 309.

Some Exchange

The first written puzzles appeared in ancient Egypt at about 1650 b.c. These puzzles were part of an 18½-foot scroll called the Rhind Papyrus. Times have changed since then, but many puzzles haven't. Just try these next ones.

Examine the two stacks of number blocks. If you exchange one block from one column with one block from the other, the number of their sums will be equal. Which blocks need to be exchanged?

Now that you know how to balance two columns, you're ready to move up to three columns! By exchanging one block from each column, each of the three blocks' sums will be equal. Remember that all three columns must undergo only one exchange.

Answers on pages 309.

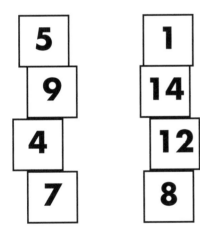

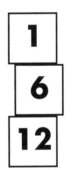
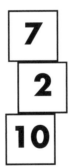
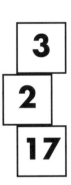

The Clues

Absolute Madness

They were received into the hospital as insane.

They had not carried out any action to indicate that they were insane.

They hadn't met before, but there was a link between them.

They had all set out to travel by bus.

Another Landlubber

He went around quite quickly.

He saw Africa, Asia, Europe, North America, and South America.

He didn't sail the ship.

Basket Case

She was very well known in her time.

She was involved in the execution of people.

She never said a word.

Bertha's Travels

Bertha is a woman who normally travels with other people.

She doesn't travel by walking or running, nor by plane or boat.

She provides a service to passengers.

Blow by Blow

He was secretly blowing darts at particular targets.

His nefarious actions generated more sales at the fairground.

Bus Lane Bonus

The bus lanes were introduced because of heavy traffic congestion. Normal traffic was forbidden to use the bus lanes so the buses could move more quickly.

The reduction in death rate wasn't due to fewer road accidents, fewer pedestrian accidents, less pollution, or fewer cars in the city.

Accident victims were saved.

Cheap and Cheerful

The fresh food was in perfectly good condition.

The man was normal and didn't have any allergies or aversions.

The food was salmon.

Chop Chop

The tree was not hazardous, harmful, or threatening in any way.

The problem does not involve animals, students, seeds, leaves, roots, or branches.

The problem related to the tree's location.

Co-lateral Damage

Some damage is fatal to a plane and some is not.

The returning planes are not a true sample of all the planes and all the damage.

U.S. bomber command used the information about damage on returning planes to strengthen planes and so reduce losses.

The Costly Wave

He wasn't at an auction.

He waved to fans and onlookers.

Criminal Assistance

The police notices were to warn people about certain types of thieves.

The thieves observed people's reactions to the signs.

The Deadly Dresser

If he had not dressed, he would not have died.

He died by accident.

He was poisoned.

The Deadly Feather

The man was physically fit and healthy.

The feather had touched him.

He was a circus performer.

The Deadly Omelet

He was a wanted man.

The omelet and its ingredients were relevant.

He had not done anything illegal.

This incident happened in France.

The Deadly Stone

The blood on the stone was the man's blood. It had been put there two days before his death.

Nobody else was involved.

He had marked the stone with his blood for a purpose.

Denise and Harry

Denise and Harry harmed people.

They weren't humans but they weren't animals either.

The Dinner Clue

The police obtained the evidence they needed.

He didn't finish his meal.

Disconnected?

The horse was alive throughout and was not exceptional.

The horse was a working horse.

The two legs that traveled farthest were the front left and back left.

Eensy Weensy Spider Farm

It was relevant that the spider farms were in France.

The spiderwebs were used, but not to catch anything.

They are found in wine-growing regions.

The Engraving

What she received wasn't what she expected.

A fine artist had created the picture she received.

The engraving had already been put to use.

Face-off

The soldiers were killed, but not in action, nor by disease, flood, storm, or fire.

It was during winter.

Some test shots were fired, but the shells fell well away from the soldiers.

Fast Mover!

The man didn't use airplanes or super-fast ground transport.

He did not need his passport.

Floating Home

The man was normal, but he had been on an extraordinary voyage.

He had not set off by sea, but he had always intended to return in the manner in which he did.

He returned safe and well. He was found by people who were concerned for his well-being.

Foreign Cure

He didn't go abroad for drugs, medicines, treatments, or cures that were unavailable in the U.S.

His illness was curable given the right motivation.

He went to an Arab country.

Forging Ahead

He used the $50 bill to help pass a forged bill—but not a forged $50 bill.

He bought something he didn't want.

Frozen Assets

The railway was needed temporarily to carry cargo to a certain location.

It was possible to lay tracks over the land to reach the place, but they were unable to do so.

They wanted to supply food and ammunition.

The Gap

He was writing in an unusual way.

The writing was important and would be seen by many people.

He was planning ahead.

The Generous General

The general felt he had been misled.

The recipient's response wasn't what the general expected.

A Geography Question

Three of the answers are routine, but one is unexpected—and lateral!

Maine isn't the most eastern state.

Half for Me and Half for You

Lucrezia Borgia's companion died of poisoning.

The apple was taken at random from a bowl of perfectly good apples.

Lucrezia deliberately killed her companion.

Hearty Appetite

The whale was a killer whale.

The whale was at sea.

The people who were disappointed hadn't come to see the whale.

High on a Hill

The man managed to stay warm but he didn't burn anything.

The man was alone. No person or animal

helped him to keep warm.

The mountain was dangerous.

History Question

September 8, 1752, was a very unusual day—but there were 10 other days like it.

No significant wars, births, deaths, disasters, achievements, or discoveries happened in London that day.

Honorable Intent

The six people had never met the seventh person and never would meet him.

The seventh person wasn't famous, remarkable, or well known.

The six people all owed a great debt to the seventh person—but not a financial debt.

Hot Job

The robber's face was covered, but he was easily identified.

His choice of clothing was poor.

Inheritance

Both sons reached the shore. The younger was judged to have touched the shore first.

The younger son took drastic action.

In the Middle of the Night

He didn't hear or smell anything that might have helped him.

The watch wasn't luminous.

None of the objects could be seen in the pitch dark.

Invisible Earnings

Nauru exports something of value.

It has nothing to do with tourism, finance, or crafts.

There are many seabirds in Nauru.

Jericho

Although he constructed it with great care, the man thought that the house might fall down.

He didn't intend that he or anyone else live in the house.

Joker

They weren't playing strip poker and stripping wasn't a forfeit or penalty involved in the game.

The actual card game isn't relevant.

She took off her clothes to avoid harm.

Knights of Old

It doesn't concern horses or weapons.

The custom has evolved and is used today by military personnel for a different purpose.

Originally it involved sight and recognition.

Landlubber

He circumnavigated the world and crossed every line of longitude.

There was nothing special about his boat or on his boat.

He sailed his boat around the world but always stayed within a few miles of shore.

He did it from November to February.

The Last Mail

There was no difference in the contents, envelope, or addressing of the two letters.

They were both sent by the same method—first class.

The same clerk at the same post office handled both letters.

The man weighed the letters and found their weights were identical. He then put stamps on them and took them to the postal clerk, who told him that one of the letters was fine but that the other needed more stamps.

Lethal Relief

They didn't die of hunger, disease, or food poisoning.

The relief was delivered to remote areas.

The people died before they opened the packages of food.

Lifesaver

Any speech of the same length would have had the same effect.

Someone made an attempt on his life.

The Man Who Did Not Fly

The fictitious person did not exist and did not fly.

The police knew about this situation.

Other passengers had been victims of a crime.

The Man Who Would Not Read

Conditions on the train were perfectly suitable for reading.

He was very obedient.

No local resident would have made the same mistake.

Material Witness

They are perfectly normal curtains and not special.

Mechanical Advantage

The problem wasn't with the engine of his car.

It was raining.

He bought something sweet and used that to solve the problem.

Mined Over Matter

The mine was live and dangerous. It would explode if it came into contact with metal.

He took some action to deflect the mine from the ship.

He did not touch or defuse the mine.

Mine Shafted

The buyer explored the mine and found the silver as was intended.

They were genuine pieces of silver but not the sort you would find in a silver mine.

Murder Mystery

Both the husband and wife had been married before.

Their marriage was successful and neither was unfaithful to the other.

She killed her husband to help someone she loved.

My Condiments to the Chef

The owner wasn't trying to save money or be more efficient.

There had been a problem involving the bottles of vinegar.

He was trying to discourage a certain group of customers.

Not Eating?

The hungry man wanted to eat and there was no medical, religious, or financial reason for him not to eat.

He was physically fit, healthy, and normal.

He was in the same room as his plate and the plate had food on it. But he wasn't able to eat it.

Not the Führer

There was no identity tag or personal effects that would have revealed the man's identity.

There were no distinguishing marks on the man's body.

His clothing gave the clue.

The Office Job

The man's age, appearance, gender, and dress didn't matter.

Everyone had completed the form correctly and in a similar fashion.

The man showed that he had a skill required for the job.

Orson Cart

The group that wasn't fooled did not know the plot of the play or the book, nor did they spot any production flaw.

They were children.

Outstanding

The feature of *The Old Farmer's Almanac* that made it more popular had nothing to do with its printed contents.

It had no value other than as an almanac.

Its advantage was practical.

Paper Tiger

The sheets of paper were important. He wrote the numbers in ink.

He intended to keep the papers for his later personal use.

He did this each year at a certain time of year.

Plane and Simple

The tree was normal and the boy was normal.

Trees grow differently from boys.

Pork Puzzler

The bacon served a purpose on the journey but was never used as food.

He packed it at the top of his suitcase.

Bacon is offensive to certain people.

Publicity Puzzler

The two men both share a problem. It's an unusual problem. It's not identical for each man.

By shopping together they gain a financial benefit.

They shop for one type of item only. It's not food, furniture, or electrical goods.

Quo Vadis?

The archaeologist didn't use any written or pictorial evidence.

He deduced that Romans drove their chariots on the left-hand side of the road from physical evidence. But not from the remains of chariots.

He excavated a Roman quarry.

Resistance

The booby traps depended on a likely action that Germans might take.

Germans have a reputation for being well organized, neat, and tidy.

Rich Man, Poor Man

It has nothing to do with the costs or prices of tea or milk.

It has nothing to do with the taste or flavor of the tea.

It concerns the cups from which they drank their tea.

Rock of Ages

He was oblivious to all around him.

He was struck with a strong blow.

His wife tried to help him.

Running on Empty

Something bad was averted.

Nobody was driving the car when it ran out of gas.

Rush Job

He exploited a different need of the miners.

He turned the tents to some other use—not accommodation.

The tents were made of heavy denim material.

School's Out

She was instructed to go to school for her education.

She was already very old (and well educated).

She was issued the court order automatically.

The Sealed Room

Nothing else and nobody else was involved except the man and the sealed room.

He died slowly but not from lack of food, water, or oxygen. If he had not been in the sealed room, he would have lived.

Shave That Pig!

The pigs were used for something other than food.

This happened only in winter.

Shell Shock

The game is rigged.

The dealer is fast, but it isn't speed alone that deceives the player.

Sick Leave

Walter was human and physically normal.

The hospital was a normal hospital.

He wasn't able to walk into the hospital or out of it.

Sign Here

He had intended to use the two signs in two places to give the same message, but he found that that didn't work.

He was advertising his roadside café.

Silly Cone

The office manager found a way to make people waste less time.

The cones were given away free.

A cone will not rest on its end.

The Single Word

Other people also heard what she had to say.

There is no sexual connotation to this story. The narrator could be male or female.

The word I said summarized a decision that would significantly affect the woman.

None of my companions was allowed to speak in the woman's presence.

Small Is Not Beautiful

It doesn't have to do with pollution, crime, economy, car production, or politics.

The reason concerned safety.

Small cars were more dangerous in certain types of accidents that occur often in Sweden.

Smile Please!

The toothpaste company adopted his idea and their sales increased.

It had nothing to do with the taste, price, or distribution of the toothpaste.

The idea encouraged people to use more toothpaste.

Spies Are Us

They went to the restaurant as paying customers.

No codes were used, and they never spoke or sat near each other.

They dressed in similar clothes.

Stamp Dearth Death

If he had bought the right postage, he would have lived.

He sent a package.

A Strange Collection

The contents are inedible, but they are not bones or animal parts.

They had done something relevant together earlier in the day.

They are eating game.

The Stuffed Cloud

The meteorologist died.

He wasn't aware of the stuffed cloud. It hadn't affected any of his forecasts or reports.

He was traveling.

Superior Knowledge

Nobody said anything, but there was visible evidence of the man's presence.

It was nothing to do with shaving.

Surprise Visit

The factory manager and his staff cleared away all the rubbish and left the factory looking spotlessly clean.

The chairman arrived in an unexpected fashion.

He saw a terrible mess.

That Will Teach You

This didn't happen at night.

He hadn't left any heating, lighting, or cooking equipment on.

The thing he had forgotten had helped cause a fire.

Throwing His Weight About

The man was normal, fit, and healthy.

He died by accident.

He was trying to demonstrate something.

Tittle Tattle

Tittles are seen in print.

There are two in this sentence.

Top at Last

William didn't cheat.

He didn't revise or work any harder than usual.

He wasn't particularly happy to be top of the list.

The Tracks of My Tires

The police didn't ask any questions but merely used their powers of observation.

When the police arrived, none of the three suspects was carrying a weapon or wearing blood-stained clothing.

The police correctly deduced that the woman was the murderer.

Turned Off

The man didn't interfere with the physical operation of the radio stations.

There was no threat or misinformation.

All radio stations voluntarily chose to stop transmitting for a short period.

2020 Vision

The farmer was being truthful.

Exactly 22 pigs were stolen.

Two Pigs

They were sold on the same day at the same market.

Each was sold for a fair price.

The two pigs looked the same, but when they were sold one was worth much more than the other.

One was sold for food—the other was not.

Unfinished Business

The work isn't necessarily big.

Many people undertake this work.

None of them can ever truly complete it.

Up in Smoke

The cigars were valuable. He didn't steal or sell them.

He was perfectly entitled to smoke them.

He successfully claimed the $10,000, and as a result was found guilty of a crime.

The Upset Bird Watcher

The bird was just as beautiful and rare as he had imagined. He wasn't disappointed with its appearance.

What happened to the bird placed him at risk.

He saw the bird through a small window.

The Upset Woman

He was an unwelcome intruder.

He had visited before, so she left some food for him.

She wanted him to die.

Vase and Means

They discovered the ingredient by accident.

The ingredient strengthened the pottery.

The accident was a tragedy.

Watch Out!

The man thought it was much later than it actually was.

It was dark when he went outside.

The man was unusual.

The Wedding Present

He was embarrassed with shame when his gift was opened.

His gift wasn't offensive to the bride and groom in any religious, political, or moral way.

He had bought an expensive gift but then made a mistake and tried to save money.

What's the Point?

A round pencil would not do.

She hates losing pencils.

Who Did It?

The teacher didn't threaten or bribe any child.

No child admitted the misdemeanor or tattled on anyone else.

The teacher gave the class an exercise to do.

Who Wants It Anyway?

It's something that can be won or lost. If you lose it, then you suffer financial and other penalties.

Wonderful Weather

The accident happened at night.

No other craft was involved.

The accident happened in winter.

Written Down

She is writing in an unusual place.

She has difficulty writing the letters P, R, T, and Z but no difficulty with O, Q, S, U, X, and Y.

She is writing on thick books.

Wrong Way

The man had a rational reason for choosing a bus going in the opposite direction to the one he wanted.

His reason was not to do with saving money, saving time, avoiding danger, seeing anything, or meeting anyone.

His reason has to do with comfort.

Acidic Action

He disposed of her clothes and jewelry.

Her body was completely dissolved in acid.

A trace of her was found and identified.

Adolf Hitler

It was the real Adolf Hitler, the one who led the German Third Reich.

Adolf Hitler was alive at the time, and the war still had much time to run.

The British soldier did not recognize Hitler. But it would have made no difference if he had.

Adrift in the Ocean

They found a source of drinking water.

No rain or ice is involved.

They were in a particular location.

Alex Ferguson

Soccer is played in Singapore.

Alex Ferguson's style of coaching would be appropriate.

One of his personal habits would not be acceptable in Singapore.

Alone in a Boat

They were deliberately cast adrift from a famous boat.

The animals can sometimes offend the senses.

Ancient Antics

It has to do with nourishment.

It does not involve a particular strength or physical skill.

It concerns animals.

Angry Response

She was angry because he was late.

They had no particular appointment at eight o'clock.

Assault and Battery

John is healthy.

The person who hits John does it to help him.

It is a common occurrence.

The Auction

He was bidding for a pet.

The creature had a talent.

He thought he was in a competitive auction.

Bald Facts

Her hair loss was part of a greater misfortune that befell her.

She did not lose her hair from natural causes.

Her choice of lover was important.

Bare Bones

The student was healthy and was not physically abnormal.

She had never had any kind of medical operation.

Every human is born with two femurs.

Barren Patch

The patch of land received the same sunlight and rain as the fertile land around it.

The patch is an irregular shape.

No one had ever gone there, but human action had made the land barren.

Biography

His death was accidental.

Had he chosen a different subject for a biography, he would not have died.

The author died a similar death to that suffered by the subject of his biography.

Bottled Up

The bottles remained unbroken, unchanged, and unused throughout.

They were worthless when empty, but had been expensive when full.

She was status-conscious.

Burnt Wood

The wood has a symbolic value, but is not in itself rare or valuable.

The men involved in this quest all speak English yet come from countries far apart.

They compete over many weeks.

Business Rivalry

Cain uses Abel's lower prices to his own personal advantage.

Cain changes his profession.

They were competitors in the early days of the railroad business.

The Carpet Seller

The solution can be accomplished in a single cut, but it is not a straight cut.

The two pieces can fit together perfectly to make either a 9 by 16 rectangle or a 12 by 12 square.

The carpet is not used on the stairs, but it may be helpful to think in terms of steps!

Cartoon Character

The scientific journal misstated and exaggerated the properties of something.

The cartoon character was designed to be a sort of role model for children, and to influence their habits.

The cartoon character was intended to make an unpopular but healthy item popular.

Chimney Problem

He came down very slowly.

The chimney was not the same after he finished his descent.

Clean-Shaven

Alexander the Great was interested in military conquest.

He believed that clean-shaven soldiers had an advantage.

Complete Garbage

If the garbage had not been emptied, he would have lived.

He was poor and tired.

He died a violent death.

Dali's Brother

Salvador Dali is recognized as a brilliant surrealist painter.

Salvador Dali's younger brother was actually a brilliant surrealist painter but his older brother never knew this.

The two brothers had something important and unusual in common.

A Day at the Races

The man deserved to be punished.

He had no special influence with the police, and they fully intended to prosecute him.

He had a special skill that he often used to his advantage.

Debugging

Ants were used in the diagnosis of diabetes.

The ants' actions could indicate that a person had diabetes.

Don't Get Up

No one else is in the apartment and she knows that no one else will answer the phone.

She does not know the caller, but she knows that the call is probably important.

She knows the call is not for her.

She has no malicious motives.

88 Too Big

It was a number he chose to use.

He was not at home.

He did not know the right number.

Exceptional Gratitude

Bill thanked Ted for eggs he had never received in order to influence Ted's actions.

They were neighbors.

Ted was lazy and mean.

Fair Fight

The boxer did not expect to collect any money.

The trainer collected a worthwhile sum for his efforts.

The boxer won fairly, but without throwing a punch.

Fill Her Up!

He deliberately ruined the car, but later he deeply regretted his action.

He was a jealous cement truck driver.

Fingerprint Evidence

It was not Bundy's fingerprints or any of his victim's fingerprints that incriminated him, but it was fingerprint evidence.

The police found something unusual when they searched Bundy's apartment.

Fired for Joining Mensa

Anne's employers would not have objected to her joining any other organization.

She was employed in an administrative position, she did her job well, and her employers were pleased with her.

If she had joined Mensa, there may have been a conflict of interest.

Flipping Pages

I did this deliberately in order to produce a specific result.

I could do this only in certain places.

I should have gotten permission from the publisher first.

Free Lunch

The man ate his lunch with one knife and one fork.

He provided a service.

The restaurant provided an intimate atmosphere in the evenings.

Full Refund

It was highly unusual for the theater to give a refund.

The theater manager was glad that they left.

They had acted cruelly.

Garbage Nosiness

I was annoyed with myself, not with my neighbors.

I looked in the cans on the same morning each week.

When I looked in the cans, I saw that they had something in common, which mine did not.

Gas Attack

He did not use the mask to disguise himself or anyone else.

The gas mask was standard issue.

His actions could have saved the lives of many people.

Getting Away with Murder

The man had a longstanding motive to kill her.

He was clearly guilty, but had to be released under the law.

He was punished for this crime.

Golf Bag

Paul removed the bag without touching it.

He did not deliberately set fire to the bag since that would have incurred a penalty.

He indulged in a bad habit.

Happy Birthday

There was nothing about his appearance that indicated it was his birthday.

He was not well known.

She worked in a shop but was not a shop assistant.

She had access to information.

Hosing Down

They used regular water. The road was not contaminated in any way.

It was for a special event.

They did not hose the entire road.

Invisible

It can be made of metal or wood.

It is powerful.

You can see it under some circumstances, but not others, even when it is directly in front of you.

Job Description

She acted on impulse, but she chose them for a specific reason.

The woman was angry because of the men's actions.

She knew they had been talking about her.

Leadfoot and Gumshoe

She and the police officer were strangers and she was not trying to help or impress him.

She was acting from high moral principles, and was also protecting someone's reputation.

Machine Forge

The man sells the machine to a crook.

Although the machine produces perfect $100 bills, it cannot be used to make the crook rich.

Man in Tights

He was knocked out by the rock, but it did not touch him.

He was involved in many dangerous adventures.

He was a well-known sight in his tights.

The Man Who Got Water

He had intended to use the water in connection with his car, but something happened to make him change his mind.

He was very angry.

Missing Items

He grows them.

Everyone has them—men and women.

They are in the lower part of the body.

Misunderstood

Very few, if any, criminals speak this language.

It is chosen for its rarity.

A handful of words are used—but they are important.

Motion Not Passed

Many people voted for the motion, and the poll was performed correctly according to the rules.

If a few more people had voted against the motion, it would have been passed. If many more people had voted against it, then it would have been rejected.

No More Bore

Churchill gave the butler something.

The butler gave the impression that he was misbehaving.

Nonconventional

They are not prohibited from speaking altogether.

The do not use signs, gestures, or codes.

They are extremely courteous and concerned for the well-being of their companions.

Nonexistent Actors

The nonexistent actors had never existed and took no part whatsoever in the movie, but their names were put deliberately into the credits.

It was a murder-mystery movie.

No Response

The question was one that he often answered, and if anyone else had asked it he would have answered.

The content of the question does not matter. It was the way it was asked that matters.

The stranger had a difficulty.

Noteworthy

The criminal had committed a crime in the woman's house.

The criminal had visited the bank.

The picture of the president is well known.

November 11

Although it appeared as though many customers had been born on November 11, the real distribution of births of the company's customers was not unusual.

All the data had been entered on a computer database.

The customers appeared to have birthdays on November 11, 1911.

Once Too Often

You can do this many times in your life.

You do it on a specific day that is not of your choosing.

It is variously considered a right, a privilege, and a duty.

One Mile

The one-mile kink is not associated with any physical or geographical feature of the landscape. The land there is the same as elsewhere along the border.

There was no mistake in the original map and none in the current map.

Actions were taken to speed up the survey of the border.

Pass Protection

Other people could pass through in the same fashion that I did.

As I looked at the people in line, I could see the frustration in their faces.

I always buy a token for every journey.

Pentagon Puzzle

The number of people working there is not relevant.

The reason dates back to when the Pentagon was built.

When it was built, the extra bathrooms were necessary.

Picture Purchase

He was honest and there were no crooked motives involved.

He did not intend to take any action to make the picture more valuable.

He would not have bought the picture if it had been rolled up.

Poor Investment

They could easily buy another of these items; in fact, they had several spare ones.

If it was lost, then it had to be found.

They were looking for information.

The Power of Tourism

The tourists do not consume large amounts of electricity.

The place does not have costly lights or

unusual electrical entertainment or appliances.

The place is a famous natural tourist attraction.

Promotion

The company knows exactly what John is like.

Promoting John is part of a clever plan.

They promote him very publicly.

The Ransom Note

The police could glean no clues from the content, paper, or style of the ransom note.

The ransom note was mailed, but the postmark gave no clues.

There were no fingerprints, but the police were able to establish a unique match with the criminal.

Reentry

It is popular.

It is a collection.

Rejected Shoes

The shoes fit him comfortably, but there was something uncomfortable about them.

They were made of different material from his other shoes.

They were fine when worn outside, but not when worn inside.

Replacing the Leaves

The girl is very sad.

She is trying to prevent something from happening.

She is acting on something she heard.

Riddle of the Sphinx

The Sphinx had poetic license. Morning, afternoon, and evening are metaphorical rather than literal times.

Not all the legs are limbs, but they all support the body.

Right Off

He is upset that his new car is ruined, but pleased at something else.

No other vehicle is involved.

He acquires something rare.

Russian Racer

The papers reported accurately, but put the most positive light on the Russian car's performance and the most negative on the American car's.

The papers did not report how many cars raced.

Scuba Do

He had not been diving and had no immediate intention of going diving.

He was an avid diver.

The reason had to do with safety.

Secret Assignment

Knowing the students' habits, he did some clever detective work.

He knew they were serious, studious, and always prepared themselves for assignments.

He checked something in a particular place at the university.

Seven Bells

The shopkeeper could easily change the sign, but chooses not to do so.

No superstition about numbers is involved.

Many people notice the discrepancy.

Shaking a Fist

The man was not a criminal. He had been driving erratically.

There was something unusual about the man.

The policeman quickly knew that the man was in danger.

Shooting a Dead Man

The policeman knew that the man was already dead.

He wanted someone else to see what he was doing.

He was not tampering with evidence. He was trying to get information.

The Shoplifter

She does not stop, because she is in danger of being caught.

She steals under a certain guise that enables her to gradually steal larger items.

She is recognized on her regular circuit, but is not known to be a shoplifter.

Six-Foot Drop

The tomato fell six feet.

It was a regular tomato.

The man was fast.

Slow Drive

There is nothing wrong with the man, the car, the road, or the driving conditions.

This happened under very particular circumstances. At other times he drives at normal speeds.

If he went faster, he would lose something he values.

Spraying the Grass

He wanted the grass to look perfect.

Something was different about the spraying this time.

If he had done this regularly, it would have eventually harmed the grass.

Statue of an Insect

The insect had caused a big problem.

The town's prosperity depends on agriculture.

The insect's actions caused a change.

Straight Ahead

It was not done for economic reasons.

The straight miles make no difference to traffic conditions.

The straight miles were designed for use in extreme circumstances.

Strangulation

She was strangled to death with a scarf.

No dancing was involved.

She should not have been in such a hurry.

Talking to Herself

The man was recording something for his archives.

She held a unique distinction.

The Test

Each boy deserved the grade he was given.

There was something unusual about the test.

Jerry was not as diligent as he should have been.

Three Spirals

It appeared as though she was receiving something for pleasure, but for her it was deadly serious.

She was involved in dangerous and illegal activities.

The spirals contained information.

Two Clocks

They were fully functional clocks that were used to measure time.

The clocks were used only occasionally and never when the man was on his own.

The man had a particular hobby.

The Unbroken Arm

She was not seeking sympathy or help. Nothing was concealed in the cast.

She was about to do something important.

She knew that the plaster cast would be noticed immediately.

Unclimbed

It is not underwater—it is clearly visible aboveground.

It would be very difficult to climb.

Unknown Recognition

The man was physically normal and there was nothing abnormal about his appearance.

I am not related to him, but a relationship is involved.

The Unlucky Bed

All the patients who died were seriously ill, but they were not expected to die.

There is nothing wrong or dangerous about the bed or its location.

No doctors or nurses are involved in the cause of the deaths.

Patients receiving particular treatment are put in this bed.

Up in the Air

It is small.

It does not fly.

Check your assumptions on every word of the puzzle!

Walking Backward

There was no one else in the house.

The man was not afraid of any danger to himself.

He did not know who had rung the bell.

He ran out the back in order to run around to the front of the house.

Waterless Rivers

This is not a physical place.

It has mountains, but you could walk over them easily.

The cities, forests, mountains, and rivers are real places on planet Earth.

Weak Case

He paid his bail fully and promptly, but paying it incriminated him.

He paid in cash, but it was untraceable.

Well-Meaning

There were several of these creatures in a public place.

They were facing death.

She made a false assumption about the conditions necessary for their survival.

Window Pain

Both the windows are perfect squares.

Their areas are different.

They look different.

Winning Numbers

If I participate, I will have the same chance as everyone else.

I am in no way prohibited from playing or winning.

The piece of paper has next week's winning lottery numbers on it. It also has last week's winning numbers.

Wiped Out

She worked as a cleaner in a large building.

She cleaned on every floor.

She did much more work than was necessary.

Wonder Horse

The horse did not deserve to win.

The weather was relevant.

This horse did not work as hard as the other horses in the race.

The Writer

It was a long process.

Somebody helped him.

He used a part of his body that was not paralyzed.

The Wrong Ball

The ball was clearly visible and accessible.

He did not touch the ball or examine it.
He knew it wasn't his immediately upon seeing it.

You Can't Be Too Careful

The pure medicine tastes very bitter.

They do not buy it as a medicine, although it is medicine.

It is effective against malaria.

Adam Had None

It has nothing to do with family, relations, bones, or physical appearance.

It has to do with names.

Appendectomy I & II

No financial gain is involved in either solution.

The doctors who removed the healthy appendixes acted out of good motives.

Both solutions involve situations in the first part of the 20th century.

Arrested Development

The robber wanted to get out of the bank as quickly as he could.

There was nothing particularly noticeable or remarkable about the bank robber that would make him easy to identify.

He was not very bright.

Arrested Development—Again

The robbers wore masks so as not to be recognized.

They made a clean getaway.

Bank employees noticed something about the two men.

The men were brothers.

Bad Trip

The anti-drug agency wanted to actively promote a message that drugs were bad, but inadvertently they ended up promoting the opposite message.

The agency distributed pencils to children and the children used them.

Bags Away

The passenger's suitcase was stored in the hold of the plane.

He was not a terrorist or criminal.

The passenger's suitcase did not contain chemicals, explosives, or drugs.

Bald Facts

Mary, Queen of Scots took great care never to be seen without her wig.

Her wig was very good and looked completely natural.

Although Mary, Queen of Scots never wanted to be seen without her wig, she was not upset or embarrassed when it eventually happened, even though many people saw it.

Body of Evidence

The woman was seen entering and leaving the police station, but no one tried to stop her.

She was not a criminal or deliberately aiding a criminal.

She was doing her job.

The Burial Chamber

The burial chamber wasn't built for use by the builder.

He wrecked it before anyone was buried there.

He did not wreck it out of spite or anger. He deliberately destroyed it in order to deceive.

He wrecked the chamber in order to save the chamber.

Caesar's Blunder

The sea was calm and there were no storms when Caesar sailed across the channel and arrived in Britain.

He arrived safely and disembarked his troops and equipment.

Caesar had never visited Britain before.

He had learned to sail in the Mediterranean.

Café Society

The café owner did not change the menu or prices or music in the café.

He changed the appearance of the café in a way that embarrassed the teenagers.

Carrier Bags

The suggestion was a way of creating new aircraft carriers much more cheaply than by the conventional methods.

It would possibly have been practical in the North Atlantic.

They were disposable carriers.

The Cathedral Untouched

The area all around St. Paul's was heavily bombed, but it appeared that no bombs could fall on St. Paul's.

The German bombers deliberately avoided bombing it.

They were not acting out of any religious or moral principles.

The Deadly Drawing

She was correct in her deduction that someone had been killed.

She did not know the person who had been killed, nor who had killed them, nor how they had died.

She had never been in that room before and she had not seen the picture before.

The Deadly Sculpture

He lived a lonely life in a remote building.

He made the statue out of copper. It was taken far away and he never saw it again.

He died as the result of an accident. No other person or animal or sculpture was involved.

Death by Romance

They did not die of food or gas poisoning, nor from the effects of any kind of exertion.

They were not murdered. They died by accident.

They were in an unusual house.

Death of a Player

The man was not involved in any collisions or tackles and did not suffer any injuries, yet it was because of his sport that he accidentally died.

He was a golfer, but he was not hit by a club or a ball or indeed by anything.

If only he had put his tee in his pocket!

Destruction

The customer was a man who accidentally destroyed the premises without knowing that he was doing so.

He was there the whole time that the premises were being destroyed.

He was very overweight.

Down Periscope

The submarine was in water at all times and was not on dry ground or in dry dock.

No water entered the submarine.

This could happen only in certain places, and not in the open sea.

Driving Away

Driving conditions were excellent, but the thief found the woman's car very difficult to drive.

She had had the car modified.

The rich woman suffered from some of the same frailties as other old people.

There was nothing unusual about the car's engine, gears, wheels, steering, or bodywork.

Election Selection

The successful candidate had no particular experience, qualifications, or characteristics that qualified him for the job or increased his appeal to voters.

He did not canvass or advertise or spend money in any way to influence the voters, and he remained unknown to the voters.

The other candidates were competent and trustworthy and did nothing to disqualify themselves.

He changed something about himself.

The Empty Machine

Kids had cheated the gum company.

They had not put quarters into the machine, but they had obtained gumballs.

The machine was rusty, but it still worked fine.

Evil Intent

It was nothing she said or did with the man. He did not remember anything to cause his realization that she planned to burgle him.

He noticed something.

While he was preparing the drinks, she did something.

He had his hands full.

The Fatal Fall

The woman wasn't a criminal, and no crime was involved.

She was quite upset to have dropped the piece of wood.

The wood was a cylinder about one foot long.

The piece of wood was not particularly valuable and could easily be replaced.

Many people saw her drop the piece of wood.

The Fatal Fish

The man died in an accident. He was not poisoned or stabbed.

No other person was involved. No crime was involved.

The man did not eat the fish. The type of fish is irrelevant. It was dead.

He was not indoors.

Generosity?

He had not intended to give any money away, and did not do so out of altruistic motives.

He was under pressure.

Genuine Article

The play was written by Shakespeare and this was proven beyond doubt.

It had been copied and written out on a computer, so there were no clues from the paper or handwriting.

No analysis of the style or content was needed to prove its authenticity.

Give Us a Hand ...

The man whose hand it was had also been looking for precious stones.

He had been forced to cut off his own hand.

To find these precious stones, men needed strong limbs, good eyes, good lungs, and great fitness.

Golf Challenge I, II & III

I. The woman's gender was no handicap.

II. The woman was more than a match for the man.

III. It was a very wet day and the golf course was flooded.

The Happy Robber

He was poor. He stole something from the bank, but it was not money.

He made no financial gain from the theft. He stole for love.

He stole a rare liquid.

The Happy Woman

Although she used a driver, she walked about four miles in the course of her tour.

She wore special shoes.

She saw many flags.

Hi, Jean!

The shop owner sold food and he wanted to present it in the best possible light.

He took action to deter and kill pests.

Holed Out

It was not a good shot that got him the hole in one.

He should have been more careful.

The golfer's ball rebounded into the hole.

Another person was involved.

Hot Picture

She loved the picture, but she deliberately had it burned. No trace of it was left.

There was no criminal intent on her part, and she did not make any financial gains.

The picture was a present.

Her husband was a motorcyclist.

Jailbreak

There was an advantage to him in escaping in the morning. It had nothing to do with light, or deliveries, or prison officer routines.

He did not want to be spotted once he was outside the prison.

He knew that his escape would be detected after about half an hour.

Judge for Yourself

The defendant's actions probably influenced the judge in his favor.

The judge was scrupulously honest and would resent any intent to bribe or influence him.

Kneed to Know

The man and his wife were in a room full of people.

She put her hand on his knee not as a sign of affection or encouragement but as an act of communication.

He gained an understanding through her actions.

Leonardo's Secret

Leonardo hid the designs in a place where he thought nobody would ever find them, but they were not buried or locked away.

People carefully stored the hidden designs for years without realizing they had them.

Lethal Action

The dead people were Africans. They didn't eat the fruit.

The Brazilian authorities' actions involved pesticides.

The Africans acted illegally. Their deaths were accidents.

The Letter Left Out

The letter that is left out is chosen not because it is rarely used but because it is easily substituted without any risk of misunderstanding.

Lit Too Well?

The authorities deliberately set up lights in fields and on roads even though people living there had not requested them and did not need them.

There was damage to fields, crops, roads, and farm animals as a result.

Overall, though, human lives were saved.

Love Letters

She didn't know the men and didn't like any of them.

She had malicious intentions.

There was potential financial gain for her.

Message Received

Envoys were thoroughly searched when they arrived at a foreign location to check for hidden messages.

The envoys did not memorize the messages or ever know or see the contents of the messages.

The messages were hidden on the person of the envoy but they could not be seen, even when the envoy was naked.

The Mighty Stone

The peasant did not suggest building over it.

He suggested a way of moving the stone, but not by pushing it or pulling it.

He used its own weight to help move it.

Miscarriage of Justice

The Italian judge tried a rebel, but released a robber.

The Italian was not in Italy when he made the judgment.

The judge, the rebel, and the robber never ate any chocolate.

The Mover

It is something you see every day.

In fact you have seen one in the last few seconds.

New World Record

She did not do anything physical.

She became the only known person to achieve a certain feat.

It was not her age alone that did this, though one would have to be old to do it.

No Charge

The arresting officer followed the correct procedure and read the man his rights. There was clear evidence of his crime. But his lawyer got him released on a clear breach of his rights.

The crime he committed is irrelevant.

He did not own any music CDs or radios.

Offenses Down

The police officers filled in their reports and forms in a different fashion, which reduced crime, but they did not fill them in any better or quicker or more accurately or with more information than before.

They filled in the reports by hand, not by computer.

The key difference was their location when they did the paperwork.

The Old Crooner

Bing Crosby himself did not take part in the action to reduce crime.

His songs were used to reduce crime.

His songs are old-fashioned and melodic, which means that some people like them and some do not.

The Parson's Pup

The fact that he is religious is not relevant.

The vicar is particular about his appearance.

Peak Performance

He had been dead for many years, so it was not possible to tell from his physical condition or clothing whether he had reached the summit.

The manner of his death is not relevant.

No camera was involved.

What would he have done had he reached the summit?

Penalty

It was a regular soccer match played in the World Cup in front of thousands of people.

The players were not criminals or terrorists—just soccer players.

The match was played in an Arab country.

Pesky Escalator

There was no one else around.

The foreign visitor saw a sign.

He was very obedient.

Poles Apart

The explorers knew that there would be no sources of food other than what they carried with them.

They did something that would not normally be considered a good idea.

Police Chase

The fast police car was right behind the criminals' vehicle and there was no other traffic or vehicle involved. The roads were clear and the weather was fine.

The getaway vehicle was a bus.

The bus driver was number seven.

Pond Life

The same environmental change would have occurred if felt hats or woolen hats had become very popular.

More silk hats were sold and fewer other hats were sold.

Fur hats were out of fashion.

Poor Investment

There were no other buildings nearby, and no buildings or roads were added or removed in the vicinity.

There were no earthquakes, floods, fires, or eruptions, and no damage by trees or vegetation.

The house had a beautiful view.

Poor Show

His performances were always a flop, but he was very successful.

He was not in comedy, music, cinema, or theater.

His most famous performance was in Mexico.

He was a sportsman.

Psychic

You see the cars after you see the woman, and you did not see her leaving the car.

There is something different in the appearance of her car.

She is carrying something.

Quick on the Draw

He had a perfectly valid ticket for that day's lottery, but he was not a prizewinner.

He saw the exact numbers on his ticket come up on the TV show.

He had a cruel wife.

Razor Attack

She meant to hurt him, and he did not defend himself.

The razor made full contact with his unprotected throat.

She could not have shaved him either.

Recognition

His Aunt Mary was not carrying a sign or wearing anything distinctive. She did not have any disabilities or characteristics that would make her stand out.

He had not arranged to meet her in a specific place or asked her to wear or carry anything in particular.

He recognized her from her facial appearance.

Riotous Assembly

The section did not have the equipment it needed to reopen.

The rioters had used everything they could lay their hands on.

The police had intervened but were driven back when the rioters threw rocks at them.

The Sad Samaritan

Jim was not robbed or deceived by the motorist in any way.

Jim tried his best to help, but failed.

The motorist was stranded.

Scaled Down

The butcher had only one turkey left.

He weighed it for the customer.

He pressed down on the scale with his thumb in order to give it an exaggerated weight.

Sex Discrimination

The prison guards were not acting in a discriminatory, sexist, or unfair fashion, but simply following procedures.

Women were more likely to fall afoul of the security equipment.

Shakespeare's Blunder

The blunder did not involve physics, chemistry, mathematics, or astronomy.

The blunder concerned the twins, Viola and Sebastian.

Shoe Shop Shuffle

The four shops have similar staffing, lighting, and security arrangements.

The shop that suffers the heaviest thefts is not in a worse part of town or in an environment that is more popular with criminals.

The shop that suffers the heaviest thefts does something different with its shoes.

Shot Dead

The woman and the strangers were neither criminals nor police.

The strangers did not see the woman and did not know that she was in the house.

The strangers were armed and were a threat to the woman.

Siege Mentality

This took place in the Middle Ages.

The defenders had plenty of food, water, and ammunition.

The attackers had catapulted rocks over the walls, but had now run out of ammunition.

Sitting Ducks

The woman loves animals and hates hunting. She does not intend to use the gun for hunting or for self-defense.

There is no criminal intent in mind.

The ducks are already dead when she shoots them.

Slow Death

Aeschylus did not trip over the tortoise or slip on it.

He did not eat it or attempt to eat it. He was not poisoned or bitten by the tortoise.

No other human was involved in his death.

Sports Mad

The sports fan was not exercising. He was not injured. He wanted the tape because of his sports obsession.

No sports equipment is involved.

He was a football fan. He followed his team fanatically but rarely got the chance to go to the games.

Stone Me!

The man was much bigger than the boy.

The stone hit the man on the head.

Many people watched.

Strange Behavior

There were many trees along the side of the road. The man had never seen or noticed this tree before.

There was something different about this tree.

His primary concern was safety.

The tree itself was not a threat to him.

Take a Fence

No other person or animal was involved.

The change in color was not caused by the sun or wind.

The change in color was caused by the rain, but every other house and fence in the area remained unchanged in color.

The Tallest Tree

The men did not use angles or shadows.

They did not climb the tree.

They measured it accurately using rope and measuring lines.

Titanic Proportions

The ship that sank was not involved in the sinking of the Titanic or the rescue operation.

Laws were passed to ensure that ships improved their safety.

One ship sank but all the passengers were saved.

Tree Trouble

The wall was successful in keeping prying people away from the tree—just as intended.

The tree died.

Trunk-ated

The policeman is able to prove that there is something suspicious in the trunk without opening it.

He suspects that there is a body in the trunk.

How do you attempt to contact a dead man?

Two Heads Are Better Than One!

They were not drunk or under any strange influence.

This happened in North America.

They had seen a creature they had never seen before.

Two Letters

He is not trying to form words or to communicate or send a message.

The man is working on a crossword puzzle.

The letters he writes are S and E.

Unhealthy Lifestyle

The man's unhealthy habits helped save him.

No other people were involved.

The woman died from poison.

The Unwelcome Guest

The neighbor liked the dog and the dog did not annoy the neighbor.

The couple gave the neighbor a fine meal.

He was horrified at what happened next.

Vandal Scandal

The authorities did not add extra security or protection for the ancient buildings.

They fooled the people who were determined to take souvenirs.

Tourists went away happy.

Watch That Man!

The wristwatch was perfectly legal and did not give the runner an unfair advantage.

The man had cheated.

The clue to his cheating was that his wristwatch had changed hands.

Weight Loss

The diet and the daily regimen were not changed. But something else about the clinic was changed, and this produced the weight loss in patients.

The change made the patients work a little harder in normal activities.

The fact that the clinic is in Japan is not particularly relevant. Similar results could have been obtained in many countries—but not in Belgium or Holland.

Well Trained

Do not take this puzzle too seriously—it involves a bad pun.

The child was correct. But why?

Wonderful Walk

Something annoying happened during the walk in the woods.

It gave the man an idea.

He invented a popular fastener.

The World's Most Expensive Car

The car was used once and is in good condition, but it has not been driven for many years.

Most people have seen it on TV, but they can't name the man who drove it.

It is not associated with any celebrity or with any remarkable historical event or tragedy, though when it was driven it was a special event at the time.

It was developed at great expense for practical use and not for show or exhibition.

Would You Believe It?

The blocks of wood were identical and so were the people (for the purposes of this puzzle), but their circumstances were not identical.

Normal forces were at work in all three cases—nothing unusual was going on.

Lateral Answers

Absolute Madness

A bus driver was told to bring 20 psychiatric patients to a mental hospital. On the way he stopped to buy a newspaper. When he got back, all his passengers had gone. So he drove up to several bus stops and collected the first 20 passengers he could find and delivered them to hospital, where he warned the staff that they would all cause trouble and claim to be sane.

Another Landlubber

He was an astronaut in a space ship.

Basket Case

She was "Madame Guillotine," the deadly invention of Joseph Guillotin that was used in France to execute people.

Bertha's Travels

Bertha is an elevator operator.

Blow by Blow

The assistant at the fairground blew darts through a concealed blowpipe to burst the balloons of children on their way home from the fair so that their parents would have to return to buy replacement balloons in order to stem the tears.

Bus Lane Bonus

Emergency vehicles and, in particular, ambulances were allowed to use the bus lanes. Ambulances reached accident victims sooner and got them to the hospital sooner so fewer of them died.

Cheap and Cheerful

The food is salmon. Previously he had choked on a bone in fresh salmon. The salt in canned salmon dissolves the bones and removes this danger.

Chop Chop

For a short time on sunny days, the shadow of the old tree covered an instrument used for recording sunshine. The instrument had been put in place on a cloudy day. Good sense prevailed and the instrument was moved instead.

Co-lateral Damage

They strengthened the parts of the aircraft that had not been hit. Antiaircraft fire is random in nature. The returning planes showed damage that had not been fatal. But this sample excludes information from the planes that had not returned and had sustained fatal damage. It was deduced that they had sustained damage on the parts not hit on the returning planes. By adding armor to the planes, overall losses were reduced.

The Costly Wave

The man was the winner of the prestigious London Marathon race. He waved to the large crowd the entire way down the finishing straightaway and, because of that, he just failed to break the record time for the marathon—thereby missing out on the $30,000 bonus prize.

Criminal Assistance

The police put up notices "Beware of Pickpockets." The pickpockets stood near a sign and noticed that when people saw it they immediately checked that their purses and wallets were safe. The pickpockets then knew where their victims carried their purses and wallets—which made them easier to steal.

The Deadly Dresser

The last thing he put on was his shoe and it contained a deadly spider that bit him, and he died soon after.

The Deadly Feather

The man was a circus sword swallower. In the middle of his act someone tickled him with the feather and he gagged.

The Deadly Omelet

The man was an aristocrat on the run from the French Revolution. He disguised himself as a peasant. When he ordered an omelet, he was asked how many eggs he wanted in it. He replied, "A dozen." No peasant would have asked for more than two or three.

The Deadly Stone

The man was lost in the desert. Without landmarks, he marked stones with a drop of blood from a cut on his hand. After two days of walking and out of water, he found a stone with blood on it. He knew that he was walking in circles and he shot himself rather than face a slower death.

Denise and Harry

Denise and Harry were hurricanes.

The Dinner Clue

The meal included a large piece of stale cheese that the suspect bit into and then left. His teeth marks were found to match a bite on the body of a murder victim.

Disconnected?

The horse worked in a mill. It walked around in a circle all day to drive the millstone. In the course of the day, its outer legs walked a mile farther than its inner legs.

Eensy Weensy Spider Farm

Spiderwebs are bought by unscrupulous wine merchants who want to give the impression that their wines are old and mature.

The Engraving

She received a used British postage stamp.

Face-off

The French tested their artillery by firing some shots into the mountains. This caused avalanches that killed many soldiers on both sides.

Fast Mover!

The man was a diplomatic courier and he visited the embassies of 30 countries, all situated in Washington. In law, an embassy is part of the country of the embassy and not part of the country in which it is situated.

Floating Home

The man was an astronaut.

Foreign Cure

The man is an alcoholic. He flies to a country where alcohol is banned by law in the hope of curing his addiction by removing the temptation.

Forging Ahead

The forger bought a cheap item with the genuine $50 bill. In the change he would usually get at least one $20 bill. He would then ask the storekeeper to change the $20 bill into two tens and switch the genuine $20 bill with a forged one of his own making. The storekeeper was less likely to check a bill he believed he had just paid out.

Frozen Assets

During World War II, the Russians built a railway line over the frozen Lake Ladoga in order to deliver supplies to the city of Leningrad, which was under siege from German forces. Its population was starving and there was no means of supply from the Russian side other than over the lake.

The Gap

The man was carving a tombstone. A husband had died and the man carved

PRAY FOR
HI M.

When the wife died, she would be buried with her husband and the engraving would be amended to

PRAY FOR
THEM.

The Generous General

The soldier thanked him by saying, "Danke schön."

A Geography Question

Hawaii is the most southern and Alaska is simultaneously the most western, most northern, and most eastern. It's the most eastern because some remote islands that are part of Alaska lie over the 180-degree line of longitude and are therefore east of the continental U.S.

Half for Me and Half for You

Lucrezia Borgia put a deadly poison on

one side of the blade of a knife. When she cut the apple, only one half was poisoned.

Hearty Appetite

After the Exxon Valdez oil spill, an enormous amount of money was spent cleansing the environment and rehabilitating oil-damaged animals. Two seals had been carefully nurtured back to good health at a cost of over $100,000, and they were released into the sea in front of an appreciative crowd. A few minutes later the crowd was horrified to see them both eaten by a killer whale.

High on a Hill

The man was marooned on a volcano that had recently erupted. He was kept alive by the heat of the melting lava.

History Question

Absolutely nothing happened in London on September 8, 1752. It was one of the eleven days dropped when the old calendar was adjusted to the new one.

Honorable Intent

The six people had all received different organs from a donor who had died in an accident. They meet to honor his memory.

Hot Job

The man wore a short-sleeved shirt and his name was tattooed on his arm.

Inheritance

The younger son took his sword and cut off his hand before hurling it ashore. Since he had touched the shore before his brother, he was able to claim his father's kingdom. (This story is told of the kingdom of Ulster, and to this day a bloody red hand is used as the symbol of the province.)

In the Middle of the Night

He turns on the light.

Invisible Earnings

Nauru exports guano, which is an excellent fertilizer. Guano comes from the droppings of seabirds.

Jericho

The man was building a house of cards.

Joker

When one player went to play a card, she knocked over a mug. The hot drink poured over the other player, who immediately jumped up and started to take her clothes off.

Knights of Old

When knights in full armor rode past the king, they would raise the visor on their helmet so that the king could see them. This action in turn became the salute that military personnel give to higher officers.

Landlubber

He sailed around the coast of Antarctica.

The Last Mail

Both letters were the same weight, a fraction under the weight at which a surcharge was charged. He put the correct postage amount in stamps on each letter. One had a single stamp of the correct value and the other had several stamps adding up to the correct value. When the letters were weighed, the one with the more stamps was over the limit and so more stamps were needed.

Lethal Relief

The food was dropped by parachute in remote areas. Several people were killed when the packages fell on them.

Lifesaver

The politician was Teddy Roosevelt, the American president. In 1912, in Milwaukee, he was shot in the chest. He was saved because the bullet was slowed as it passed through the folded manuscript of the speech in his breast pocket. He went on to make the speech later on the same day that he was shot!

The Man Who Did Not Fly

In this true case, many vacationers who flew with a certain airline had their homes burglarized while they were away. The police added a false name (but real address) to the list and caught the burglar red-handed when he broke in. It turned out that his sister worked for the airline and passed the list of passenger addresses to her nefarious brother.

The Man Who Would Not Read

He saw a notice on the side of the carriage that said, "This carriage is not for Reading." Reading is a town on the main line between London and Bristol.

Material Witness

They are on the window!

Mechanical Advantage

It was raining heavily and the man discovered a leak in the roof of his car. He bought several packs of chewing gum, chewed them, and then used the gum as a waterproof filler until he could reach a garage.

Mined Over Matter

The sailor used the water hose on the ship to direct a jet of water onto the mine to push it out of the path of the ship.

Mine Shafted

He had shredded real silver dollars to produce the silver. One piece was found with the word "unum" (from "e pluribus unum") on it.

Murder Mystery

The man and woman lie badly injured after a car accident. The wife knows that they are both going to die and she fears that she will die first. They recently married and have no children from this marriage but each has children from a previous marriage. If she dies first, then all of the joint estate will go to his children. She kills her husband so that her children will inherit the entire estate.

My Condiments to the Chef

Drug addicts were using his café and dipping their needles into his vinegar bottles because heroin is soluble in vinegar. He replaced the vinegar bottles with small packets of vinegar in order to stop the addicts from dipping their syringes into the bottles.

Not Eating?

His plate is his dental plate.

Not the Führer

When the shoes were removed from the body, the man was found to be wearing darned socks. The soldiers did not believe that the Führer of the Third Reich would wear darned socks.

The Office Job

This happened in the 1800s. The man had applied for a job as a telegraph operator. Among the background noise was a Morse code message saying, "If you understand this, walk into the office." It was a test of the candidates' skill and alertness. He was the only candidate who passed.

Orson Cart

Orson Welles's voice was recognized by the many children who listened to his regular children's radio show.

Outstanding

The Old Farmer's Almanac had a hole in the top left corner that made it ideal for hanging on a nail in the outhouse.

Paper Tiger

It's January and he is writing the date of the year on all the checks in his checkbook to avoid putting last year's date by mistake.

Plane and Simple

The boy will be six inches taller than the nail. The tree grows from the top, so the nail won't rise.

Pork Puzzler

The man was traveling to a strict Muslim country where alcohol was banned. He placed a small bottle of whiskey under a pack of bacon in his suitcase. He knew that if the customs officials at the airport of entry opened his suitcase they wouldn't touch the bacon and therefore his whiskey would be safe.

Publicity Puzzler

The man has feet of different sizes—his left foot is 12 and his right foot is 13. He advertises to find a man with the opposite—a left foot size 13 and right foot size 12. Together they go shopping to find a shoe style that suits them both. They then buy two pairs, one 12 and one 13, before swapping shoes.

Quo Vadis?

The archaeologist was excavating a Roman quarry. The ruts in the road leading from the quarry were much deeper on the left than on the right. Since the carts leaving the quarry were much heavier than those returning, he deduced that the Romans drove on the left side of the road.

Resistance

Pictures in buildings that would be occupied were hung at a slight angle and attached to bombs. The tidy Germans straightened the pictures with fatal results.

Rich Man, Poor Man

Rich people had bone china that could take the hot tea, but poor people had cheap crockery that would crack if hot tea were poured into it. Pouring the tea first became a sign of prosperity.

Rock of Ages

The man was listening to rock-and-roll music through his Walkman headphones in the kitchen. He had his hand on the kettle and his back to the door. When his wife came in, she saw him shaking violently but she heard no sound. She called to him but he didn't hear her. Thinking that he was suffering from an electric shock, she picked up a rolling pin and hit his arm, breaking it.

Running on Empty

Mr. and Mrs. Jones had had a silly argument. Mrs. Jones stormed out and the depressive Mr. Jones had tried to commit suicide by sitting in his car in the garage with the engine running. He passed out, but then the car ran out of gas and when Mrs. Jones returned she rescued him and they were reconciled.

Rush Job

He used the tough tent cloth to make trousers for the miners. His name was Levi Strauss.

School's Out

She has just celebrated her 105th birthday, but the computer at the local education authority cannot recognize a date of birth that is over 100 years ago. Calculating that she is 5 years old, the computer prints out an automatic instruction to attend school.

The Sealed Room

He died from carbon dioxide poisoning, which takes effect before oxygen starvation.

Shave That Pig!

In China, live pigs were used like hot-water bottles to keep people warm in bed on cold nights. For the sleepers' comfort, the pigs were shaved first.

Shell Shock

The pea isn't under any of the shells. It's slipped under a shell by the operator as he lifts it. Sometimes the operator places the pea under a player's choice to encourage dupes.

Sick Leave

Walter was a newborn baby.

Sign Here

He bought two identical signs for his café, but found that he needed two different ones for the two sets of traffic coming in different directions. The two signs said:

"FRED'S CAFÉ >" and "< FRED'S CAFÉ"

Silly Cone

Drinking cups in the shapes of cones were provided at water fountains. Since they couldn't be put down, people had to quickly drink the water. This sped up their breaks.

The Single Word

The word was "Guilty." I was foreman of the jury at the woman's trial.

Small Is Not Beautiful

Small cars were banned in Sweden because of the high incidence of accidents involving collisions with moose. Occupants of small cars suffered serious injuries, but large cars offered more protection.

Smile Please!

The man suggested that they make the hole in the top of the tube bigger so that more toothpaste would be squeezed out each time.

Spies Are Us

The German spies wore identical hats with secret information hidden inside the hatband. They entered the restaurant at slightly different times and placed their hats on the hatrack where they could see them. They left at different times—each taking the other's hat.

Stamp Dearth Death

The man was a terrorist letter-bomber. He sent a letter bomb, but didn't put enough stamps on it. It was returned to him and it exploded, killing him.

A Strange Collection

The guests are eating pheasant, which they shot earlier that day. The container is for the pellets of lead shot.

The Stuffed Cloud

A stuffed cloud, in pilot slang, is a cloud with a mountain in it. The meteorologist was a passenger on a plane that hit a stuffed cloud. He was killed and had to be replaced at his job.

Superior Knowledge

One of the toilet seats had been left up.

Surprise Visit

The manager and staff dumped all the trash on the flat roof of the factory so that it wouldn't be seen. Unfortunately, the company chairman arrived by helicopter and landed on the roof.

That Will Teach You

The man left his glasses on his bedside table. They had focused the rays of the sun onto his pillow and started a fire that destroyed his house.

Throwing His Weight About

He was demonstrating how strong the glass was to a group of visitors. He threw himself against it, but it was not as strong

as he had thought.

Tittle Tattle

A tittle is the dot on an i.

Top at Last

William's name was William Abbott, and the results were given in alphabetical order.

The Tracks of My Tires

The woman was the only person in a wheelchair.

Turned Off

The man was Guglielmo Marconi, the pioneer of radio transmission. When he died in 1937, all the radio stations in the world observed a minute of silence as a mark of respect.

2020 Vision

As he talked to the farmer on the phone, the newspaper editor realized that the man had a slight lisp and that what he had actually reported stolen was "two sows and twenty pigs."

Two Pigs

This happened in France. One pig was sold for bacon. The other had been painstakingly trained to sniff out truffles and was therefore very valuable.

Unfinished Business

His autobiography.

Up in Smoke

In this true story, the cigars were insured under the man's general household policy as named items. He claimed against his insurance company on the grounds that the cigars had been destroyed in a series of small fires. The insurance company rejected the claim, pointing out that he had started the fires in order to smoke the cigars. He took the insurance company to court and won the case. The judge ruled that the insurance policy covered against loss by fire and that this was what had happened. The man was awarded $10,000. However, as he left the court he was arrested by the police on a charge of arson, based on his sworn testimony. He was found guilty and given a one-year suspended prison sentence.

The Upset Bird Watcher

The ornithologist was sitting on a plane coming in to land when he saw the rare bird, which was sucked into the jet engine causing the engine to fail and the plane to crash-land.

The Upset Woman

He was a mouse caught in a mousetrap.

Vase and Means

Bone china was discovered when an unfortunate worker fell into the kiln and became part of the product. Animal bones are used nowadays.

Watch Out!

The man is Count Dracula, who leaves his house for his nightly drink of blood. However, his watch has stopped and what he thinks is night is actually a solar eclipse. He is caught in the sunlight and dies.

The Wedding Present

The man selected a beautiful crystal vase in a gift shop, but he knocked it over and broke it. He had to pay for it, so he instructed the shop to wrap it and send it anyway. He assumed that people would think that it had been broken in transit. Unfortunately for him, the shop assistant carefully wrapped every broken piece before sending the package.

What's the Point?

The woman is a carpenter who works on scaffolding at a building site. A conventional round pencil is more likely to roll off and fall.

Who Did It?

One of the words that was not rude was spelled incorrectly (for example, "The headmaster is a horribul %$@*&@!"). The teacher gave a spelling test that included the word and the guilty child spelled it wrong again.

Who Wants It Anyway?

A lawsuit.

Wonderful Weather

The ship was the Titanic, which hit an iceberg on a fine night when the sea was very flat. If the weather had been worse, then the lookouts would have seen waves hitting the iceberg or heard the iceberg. (Icebergs make groaning noises when they move.) Unfortunately the iceberg wasn't seen and the rest is history.

Written Down

She is writing along the top of a closed book—on the top of the pages. Any letter with a horizontal line in it is difficult, since the pen tends to slip down between the pages.

Wrong Way

The bus from Alewife to Zebedee is always full by the time it reaches the man's stop, so he catches one going the opposite way in order to get a seat on the bus for the return journey to Zebedee.

Acidic Action

The woman's body was completely dissolved, but she had a plastic tooth that was not soluble in the acid.

Adolf Hitler

This apparently true incident took place during the first World War when Adolf Hitler was a private in the German army. He was wounded and the British soldier thought it would be unchivalrous to kill him.

Adrift in the Ocean

They are in the vicinity of the mouth of the Amazon River. The outflow of river water is so huge that the Atlantic Ocean in that region consists of fresh water for hundreds of miles.

Alex Ferguson

Alex Ferguson chews gum incessantly during soccer games. The sale and use of chewing gum are illegal in Singapore.

Alone in a Boat

The two animals were skunks that had been ejected from Noah's Ark because of the stench they were causing.

Ancient Antics

No new species of animal has been domesticated in the last 4000 years. The ancients domesticated dogs, cats, cows, sheep, horses, etc.

Angry Response

The man had said he would be home at 8:00 p.m. He arrived the following morning at 8:02 a.m.

Assault and Battery

John is a newborn baby. The doctor slaps him to make him cry and use his lungs.

The Auction

The man was bidding for a parrot that was such a good mimic that it bid against him!

Bald Facts

The woman was French and fell in love with a German officer during the German occupation of France. After the liberation, a mob shaved off all her hair and branded her a collaborator.

Bare Bones

The student was pregnant. She had two femurs of her own, two of her unborn baby, and one in her hands.

Barren Patch

Years earlier a troubled airplane had dumped its fuel onto this patch of land.

Biography

The author wrote the biography of Marie Curie, the great French scientist who made many important discoveries concerning radioactivity. She won two Nobel prizes but died of leukemia caused by radiation. The biographer collected many of her writings, belongings, and experimental apparatuses to help him write about her. Unfortunately, most of the memorabilia were highly contaminated with radioactivity, and he died later as a result of being exposed to it.

Bottled Up

She took home the man's empty champagne bottles after a party. She then left them out with her garbage for collection in order to impress her neighbors.

Burnt Wood

Every two years England plays Australia at cricket for the "Ashes." Its name stems from an epitaph published in 1882 following Australia's first victory over England. The article lamented the death of English cricket and stated that its remains would be cremated. The following year the ashes of a burnt cricket stump were presented in an urn to the captain of the English team. The urn has remained ever since at Lord's Cricket Club in London. Each "Ashes" series consists of five or six five-day matches that are fiercely contested and generate a huge following in both countries.

Business Rivalry

Cain and Abel were rival train operators involved in the shipping of cattle by rail. When Abel lowered his shipping rates well below cost, Cain dropped out of the rail business and instead bought all the cattle he could find, making a fortune by shipping them to market on Abel's trains.

The Carpet Seller

The cut is made, in feet, as shown below.

Cartoon Character

The cartoon character who owes his existence to a misprint in a scientific journal is Popeye. He was invented to encourage children to eat spinach, which was thought to contain large amounts of iron. But this information was based on an error in a scientific journal—the decimal point had been put in the wrong place, making the iron content of spinach appear ten times higher than it actually was.

Chimney Problem

The man on the tall chimney had a penknife in his pocket. With this he pried loose a brick from the top layer. He used the brick as a hammer. In this way, he gradually demolished the chimney by knocking out all the bricks and lowered himself to the ground.

Clean-Shaven

Bearded men could be grabbed by the beard in close combat.

Complete Garbage

The man was sleeping in a garbage can that was taken to the compactor.

Dali's Brother

Salvador Dali died at age 7. Nine months later his brother was born and was also named Salvador. It was the younger Salvador Dali who became the famous surrealist painter.

A Day at the Races

The man was a thief who had made money at the races by picking pockets. After the policeman took down all his details, the man picked the policeman's pocket. The policeman returned to the station with no written record. He didn't remember the details because he didn't think he would need to remember them.

Debugging

If ants gathered around the place where a person had urinated, it was a strong indication that the person had diabetes. The ants were attracted by the sugar in the urine.

Don't Get Up

The woman lives in an apartment building. She hears the phone ringing in the adjacent apartment. She knows that her neighbor, who is a brain surgeon, is out.

88 Too Big

The man was an English tourist in the U.S. He was alone in an apartment when he had a heart attack. He crawled to the phone and dialed the English emergency number, 999, instead of the 911 used in America.

Exceptional Gratitude

Bill and Ted were neighbors. Ted kept chickens. Ted's chickens had been wandering through a gap in his fence and pecking around in Bill's garden. They had never laid an egg there. But after Bill thanked Ted for the eggs that his chickens had laid, Ted quickly fixed the fence to stop the chickens from getting out.

Fair Fight

The boxer was a dog that had just won the championship at a dog show.

Fill Her Up!

The woman saved carefully and bought her husband the car as a surprise anniversary present. She had it delivered into their driveway and completed the paperwork with the salesman who brought it. Her husband was a cement truck driver.

He was jealous and suspicious. He came home unexpectedly, and when he saw the new car in his driveway and his wife talking to a smartly dressed stranger, he assumed the worst. He reversed his truck and dumped his truck's load into the car.

Fingerprint Evidence

When Bundy's apartment was searched, none of his fingerprints were found. This fact was used by the prosecution as evidence of his compulsion to clean fingerprints in all situations—showing his guilt.

Fired for Joining Mensa

Anne works for Mensa in the administration of admission tests. Under Mensa's constitution, no member can be an employee.

Flipping Pages

I was photocopying the book.

Free Lunch

The man was a piano tuner who had come to tune the piano in the restaurant. He brought his own tuning fork. The restaurateur repaid the service with a free lunch.

Full Refund

The couple had a little baby with them. They were allowed into the theater on the condition that they leave if the baby cried, with their money refunded. After about 20 minutes, they realized that the movie was terrible, so the mother pinched her baby to make it cry. They left with a refund.

Garbage Nosiness

On our street we put the cans out on the curb for collection every Monday morning. I forgot to put the can out two weeks in a row. Looking in my neighbor's can was the easiest way to confirm that I had missed the collection.

Gas Attack

The unfortunate man was August Jager who had served in the German army in World War I. He was sentenced to ten years' imprisonment in 1932 for treason. He had deserted in 1915 and been taken by the French just before the Germans launched the first-ever poison gas attack. The French asked him what his gas mask was and he told them. Ironically, it was only in 1930, when the French General Ferry wrote his memoirs, that it was revealed that Jager had told the French about the impending attack. The French ignored the information and took no evasive action. However, the German court found Jager guilty of treason in view of the fact that he had not thrown away his gas mask.

Getting Away with Murder

Many years earlier, the man's wife had faked her own murder and had run off with her lover. The man had been tried for her murder and convicted. He had served a 20-year sentence. When released, he found her and shot her, but he could not be convicted of the same crime twice.

Golf Bag

To deliberately ignite the paper bag would be to interfere with his lie and incur a penalty. So while he pondered the problem he smoked a cigarette. He discarded the cigarette onto the bag and it burned. No penalty was incurred.

Happy Birthday

The man went to the eye doctor to have an eye test. The doctor looked at his record and noticed that today was his birthday.

Hosing Down

This incident occurred just before the start of the Monaco Grand Prix race, which is held in the streets of Monte Carlo. Part of the course runs through a tunnel. When it rains outside, the firemen hose down the road in the tunnel in order to make the surface wet. This improves consistency and safety.

Invisible

The object is an airplane propeller, which rotates so fast that it cannot be seen.

Job Description

The two men were sitting by the window in the restaurant. As the woman passed, one of the men made sexist remarks to the other man, implying that the woman made her living by immoral means. She stormed into the restaurant and went up to them and said, "Actually, I am a lipreader."

Leadfoot and Gumshoe

The woman is the wife of the chief of police. In order to avoid any impression of favoritism she accepted the ticket and paid the fine.

Machine Forge

This true story concerns a confidence trickster. He sells the machine to a crook claiming it will generate perfect forgeries. He demonstrates the machine by feeding in green paper. But this green paper is actually genuine $100 bills covered in thick green coloring. The machine simply removes the green coloring.

Man in Tights

The man was Superman. He was lying next to a block of kryptonite, the one thing that could knock him out.

The Man Who Got Water

This is a true story from Russia. The man had intended to wash his car, but when he returned he found that it had been stolen.

Missing Items

The 10-year-old boy has kneecaps, which babies do not have. These develop between the ages of 2 and 5.

Misunderstood

The instructions given to police dogs are normally in a language not often spoken in the U.S., such as Hungarian or Czech. This is to make it unlikely that any person other than the trained police officers will be able to control the dog.

Motion Not Passed

Although 35% of the people voted for the referendum motion and 14% against, there were not enough votes overall for a quorum to be reached. It needed 50% of the population to vote in order for the results to be valid. If another 1% had voted against the motion, it would have carried.

No More Bore

Winston Churchill told his butler to go to the door smoking one of Churchill's finest cigars.

Nonconventional

If a nun wants the salt, she asks the nun nearest the salt if she would like the mustard, which is near the first nun. The second nun would reply, "No, but do you want the salt?"

Nonexistent Actors

The movie is Sleuth, starring Laurence Olivier and Michael Caine only. If moviegoers were not fooled into thinking that there were other actors involved, it would give the plot away. At one stage Caine leaves and returns in disguise.

No Response

The man had a stutter. The stranger who asked him the question also had a stutter. The man thought that if he answered and stuttered, then the stranger would think that he was being mocked, so the man decided not to answer.

Noteworthy

A burglar had broken into the woman's house and taken all her savings. In trying to collect the last bill that was stuffed into a jar, he tore it in half. She reported the incident to the police, and then took the half of the bill to her bank. They told her that a man had been in that morning with the matching half!

November 11

When data entry clerks entered customer records onto the computer, the date field had to be completed. However, they often did not have that data, so they simply keyed in 11/11/11.

Once Too Often

Voting twice in the same election is electoral fraud—a serious offense.

One Mile

When it was originally surveyed, two teams were sent out down the west side of South Dakota. One started from the north and one from the south. They missed! It was easier to put the kink in the border than to redo the survey.

Pass Protection

I am describing the end of my journey. My destination is a subway station that is a starting point for many commuters. I bought and used a token at the start of my trip. I simply exit through the turnstiles, passing the lines of commuters coming in.

Pentagon Puzzle

The Pentagon was built in the 1940s, when the state of Virginia had strict segregation laws requiring that blacks and whites use different bathrooms.

Picture Purchase

The picture was worthless, but it was in a fine frame that he intended to reuse.

Poor Investment

The object is the black box flight recorder from a crashed jetliner.

The Power of Tourism

The place is Niagara Falls, where the water can be diverted from the falls in order to power generators. If the beautiful view of the waterfall were not demanded by the tourists, then much of the water could be channeled through turbines to provide electricity, thus lowering the price.

Promotion

John was promoted very publicly. He was immediately headhunted by a rival firm, and lured away with a salary he could not resist. The original company wanted to fire him, but that would have been costly. They knew that their rivals were desperate to recruit one of their top people. This way, they got rid of him and saddled their rivals with a dud.

The Ransom Note

The police were able to get a DNA trace from the saliva on the back of the stamp. This matched the suspect's DNA.

Reentry

The Guinness Book of Records, after 19 years of publication, became the second-best-selling book of all time and therefore got into itself.

Rejected Shoes

The man found that the synthetic shoes generated a buildup of static electricity when he wore them around his carpeted office. He constantly got electric shocks, so he rejected them and went back to his old leather shoes.

Replacing the Leaves

The girl has a fatal disease. She overheard the doctor tell her mother that by the time all the leaves have fallen from the trees she will be dead.

Riddle of the Sphinx

The answer is man, who crawls on all fours as a child, walks on two legs as an adult, and uses a walking stick in old age.

Right Off

In this true incident, the car had been struck and destroyed by a large meteorite that the man found lying next to the car. The meteorite was rare and it was bought by a museum for over one million dollars.

Russian Racer

The Russian newspaper reported (correctly) that the American car came in next to last while the Russian car came in second.

Scuba Do

The man, who was nearsighted, was on a diving vacation. He had broken his glasses and wore the diving mask, which had prescription lenses, in order to see properly.

Secret Assignment

Ulam went to the university library and examined the library records of all the books borrowed by his students over the previous month. Los Alamos was a common link to nearly all of them.

Seven Bells

It was originally a mistake, but the shopkeeper found that so many people came into his shop to point out the error that it increased his business.

Shaking a Fist

The man suffered from severe allergic reactions to certain foods. He had inadvertently eaten something that had caused him to have a fit while driving. He veered across the road and came to a stop. He was unable to speak, but waved his hand at the policeman. He was wearing a bracelet indicating his condition. The policeman was therefore able to call for appropriate medical help.

Shooting a Dead Man

This puzzle is based on an incident in the film The Untouchables. There had been a shootout at a house and the police had captured a gangster who was refusing to give them the information they wanted. Sean Connery went outside and propped up against the window the body of another gangster, who had died earlier. Pretending the man was alive, he threatened him and then shot him. The prisoner was then convinced that Connery would stop at nothing to get the information he wanted. The prisoner talked.

The Shoplifter

The shoplifter is a woman who pretends to be pregnant. She has a whole range of false "bellies" under her coat. After nine months, she naturally has to stop.

Six-Foot Drop

He caught it just above the ground.

Slow Drive

The man was moving. He was a beekeeper. In his car he had a queen bee. His swarm of bees was flying with the car to follow the queen bee.

Spraying the Grass

This happened just prior to the 1996 Atlanta Olympics. The groundskeeper sprayed the grass with organic green paint in order to make it look greener for the television audiences.

Statue of an Insect

The insect is the boll weevil, which wreaked havoc with the local cotton crop. As a result, many of the farmers switched to growing peanuts—and became very rich when peanut prices rose.

Straight Ahead

The straight sections were specified so that they could be used as aircraft landing strips in case of war or emergency.

Strangulation

The famous dancer was Isadora Duncan, who was strangled when the long scarf she was wearing caught in the wheel of her sports car.

Talking to Herself

The woman was 87. The language she was speaking was dying out and she was the last person to know it. The man was an academic who filmed her to record the language before it was lost forever. (This puzzle is based on the true story of Dr. David Dalby's filming the last woman to speak the African language of Bikya.)

The Test

The final instruction in the test was to ignore all the previous questions. The teacher had repeatedly told the students to read over the entire exam before beginning. The test was given to see how well the pupils could follow instructions.

Three Spirals

The woman was a spy. She received record albums in the mail. When they were intercepted, they were found to contain music. However, one side had two separate spirals, one inside the other. The inner groove contained the secret information. She was caught when the authorities noticed that one side of the record lasted only half as long as the other.

Two Clocks

The man was an avid chess player. His wife gave him a chess clock. This consists of two identical clocks in one housing. Each clock records the time taken by one player for his moves in a competitive chess game.

The Unbroken Arm

The healthy young girl put a cast on her arm before going to take a French oral examination. She figured (correctly) that the examiner would ask her about her injury. She came to the exam prepared with answers about how she broke it.

Unclimbed

The largest-known extinct volcano is Mons Olympus on Mars.

Unknown Recognition

He was the identical twin brother of someone I knew well. I had heard of him but had never met him before.

The Unlucky Bed

Every Friday morning, a cleaning woman comes to the ward with a vacuum cleaner. The most convenient electrical socket is the one to which the patient's life support machine is connected. She unplugs this for a few minutes while she does her work. The noise of the vacuum cleaner covers the patient's dying gasps. The cleaner reconnects the machine and goes to the next ward. (Although this story was reported as factual in a South African newspaper, it is almost certainly an urban legend.)

Up in the Air

A dead centipede!

Walking Backward

The man walked backward from the front door as he varnished the wooden floor. He left the front door open for ventilation. When someone rang the doorbell, he quickly ran around to the front of the house in order to stop the person from walking inside onto the wet varnish.

Waterless Rivers

A map.

Weak Case

The police charged the man with stealing coins from a vending machine. He was given bail of $400, which he paid for entirely in quarters.

Well-Meaning

The animal rights activist went into a restaurant where there were live lobsters in a tank. She bought them all to liberate them, but freed them into fresh water, where they all died because they can live only in salt water.

Window Pain

Initially the square window has sides of about 1.4 feet and an area of 2 square feet. It is as shown below. The second window has sides of 2 feet and an area of 4 square feet.

Winning Numbers

One has to choose six numbers from 60 for the lotto jackpot. My piece of paper contains all 60 numbers, so it must contain the winning numbers.

Wiped Out

The woman had been told to clean the elevators in a skyscraper. She had cleaned the same elevator on each floor!

Wonder Horse

In this true story, the race consisted of three laps. It was a very misty day. One of the horses stopped at the far side, of course, waited a lap for the other horses to come around, then rejoined the race and won. The jockey later confessed.

The Writer

He winked one eye and thereby indicated to a very dedicated assistant each letter, word, and sentence of the book. He was Jean-Dominique Bauby, the French writer. The book he wrote by blinking, The Diving Bell and the Butterfly, was published just before his death in 1996 and became a bestseller.

The Wrong Ball

It had been a cold night and the ball was lying in a small frozen puddle.

You Can't Be Too Careful

The medicine is quinine, which is used to treat malaria and which people buy in tonic water. The British in India suffered badly from malaria until it was discovered that quinine cured and prevented it. Quinine tasted unpleasant, so they put it into carbonated water and created tonic water.

Adam Had None

The letter e.

Appendectomy I

The patient was a man who was going on a polar expedition in the first years of the 20th century. If he got appendicitis in such a remote region, he would die due to lack of treatment, so his healthy appendix was removed as a precaution.

Appendectomy II

Shell shock was not recognized as a genuine medical condition during World War I. Sympathetic surgeons often removed perfectly healthy appendixes from shell-shock victims so they could be sent home on medical grounds.

Arrested Development

The bank robber dashed to the revolving door and tried to push it in the direction in which it would not revolve.

Arrested Development—Again

Bank employees noticed that the two men were Siamese twins. This reduced the number of suspects dramatically.

Bad Trip

The anti-drug agency distributed pencils that had TOO COOL TO DO DRUGS printed on them. As the children sharpened the pencils down, the message became—COOL TO DO DRUGS and eventually just DO DRUGS.

Bags Away

The passenger's pet dog escaped from his suitcase in the hold and bit through some of the plane's electric cables, thereby disrupting the plane's controls.

Bald Facts

After Mary, Queen of Scots had been beheaded, the executioner held up her head to show it to the mob. The head fell out of the wig.

Body of Evidence

The woman is a cleaner who wipes the fingerprints from a murder weapon in the course of her dusting.

The Burial Chamber

The man was building the burial chamber of an Egyptian pharaoh in ancient times. He built the real burial chamber deep inside a pyramid. He also built another burial chamber that was easier to find that he deliberately wrecked so that when any future graverobbers found it, they would think that earlier graverobbers had found the tomb and taken the treasure.

Caesar's Blunder

Since the tides in the Mediterranean are very weak, Julius Caesar did not beach his ships high enough when he landed on the shores of England. Many ships floated off on the next tide and were lost.

Café Society

The café owner installed pink lighting that highlighted all the teenagers' acne!

Carrier Bags

It was seriously proposed that the British Navy tow icebergs from the north and shape the tops to serve as aircraft carriers. They could not be sunk, lasted quite a long time, and could be cheaply replaced. However, it was too lateral a solution for the Navy high command!

The Cathedral Untouched

On a moonlit night, the dome of St. Paul's cathedral acted like a shining beacon to guide German planes during the blackout, so they deliberately avoided bombing it.

The Deadly Drawing

She entered the room and saw the chalk picture outline of a body on the floor. It was the site of a recent murder and the chalk marked the position of the body.

The Deadly Sculpture

He lived in a tower on a hill. Being poor, he had no money for materials, so he took the copper lightning rod from the building. He made a beautiful statue with the copper, but soon afterward the tower was struck by lightning and he was killed.

Death by Romance

The couple spent their honeymoon on a trip to the Arctic. They stayed in an igloo. The fire melted a hole in the roof and they died of exposure.

Death of a Player

The man was a golfer who absentmindedly sucked on his tee between shots. The tee had picked up deadly weed killer used on the golf course, and the man died from poisoning.

Destruction

The body of a very overweight man is being cremated. There is so much fat that the crematorium catches fire and is burned down.

Down Periscope

The submarine started at sea and then sailed into a canal system, where each lock dropped the water level by 30 feet.

Driving Away

The rich woman was very nearsighted, but did not like wearing glasses or contact lenses. So she had her windshield ground to her prescription. The thief could not see clearly through it.

Election Selection

The successful candidate changed his name to "None of the Above." His name appeared on the list below the other candidates (Davies, Garcia, and Jones). The voters in the deprived area resented all the established political parties and voted for None of the Above as a protest.

The Empty Machine

Kids had poured water into molds the size of quarters. The molds were placed in the deep freeze and the resulting ice coins were used in the machine. They subsequently melted and dripped out of the machine leaving no trace.

Evil Intent

The man happened to put his door key in his mouth (because he was holding lots of other things in his hands). The key tasted of soap. He deduced correctly that his visitor had taken an impression of the key in a bar of soap in order to make a duplicate key so that he could be burgled.

The Fatal Fall

The woman was running in the Olympics in her national relay team. She dropped the baton and her team ended up losing. When she later returned to her country, the tyrannical despot who ran it was so displeased that he had her shot.

The Fatal Fish

The man's boat had capsized and he was adrift in an inflatable dinghy in a cold ocean. He caught a fish and, while cutting it up, his knife slipped and punctured the dinghy.

Generosity?

The man robbed a bank and was chased on foot by the public and the police. He threw away much of the cash he had acquired, which caused some chasers to stop to pick up the money and caused a rumpus that delayed the police and allowed the criminal to escape. The people who picked up the bills were forced to give them back or face prosecution.

Genuine Article

The play was written by Brian Shakespeare, a contemporary dramatist. He vouched for its authenticity.

Give Us a Hand ...

The man was a diver searching for pearls in giant clams. A previous diver had had his hand trapped in the clam, and as his oxygen ran out the poor man was forced to cut off his own hand.

Golf Challenge I

The woman's handicap was more than two shots greater than the man's.

Golf Challenge II

They were playing match play. The woman won more holes than the man.

Golf Challenge III

They were playing darts—highest score with three darts.

The Happy Robber

The man was robbing a blood bank. He stole some rare blood that his sick daughter needed for a life-saving operation. He could not have afforded to buy the blood.

The Happy Woman

She was playing golf and hit an eagle—two under par and a very good score.

Hi, Jean!

The shop owner introduced an electric insect zapper to kill flies and other insects that might land on the food. However, when the flies were "zapped," they were propelled up to five feet, and often fell on the food.

Holed Out

The golfer's ball rebounded off the head of another golfer who was crossing the green. The ball bounced into the hole. However, the man who was hit died.

Hot Picture

The woman commissioned a tattoo artist to produce a beautiful tattoo on her husband's back as a birthday present. The picture was fine, but the next day the unfortunate man was killed in a motorcycle accident. He was cremated.

Jailbreak

The man knew that his escape would be detected after about half an hour. He escaped at 10:30 on Tuesday morning just 30 minutes before the routine weekly alarm test, when everyone in the surrounding area would ignore the siren.

Judge for Yourself

The defendant sent the judge a cheap box of cigars and included the plaintiff's name card in it!

Kneed to Know

The wife of the deaf Thomas Edison used to go with him to the theater. She drummed out on his knee in Morse code with her fingers what the actors were saying on stage.

Leonardo's Secret

Leonardo hid the secret designs by painting over them with beautiful oil paintings. He knew that no one would remove such masterpieces. But he did not know that modern x-ray techniques would allow art historians to see through the oil paintings and reveal his designs.

Lethal Action

The Brazilian customs authorities require that all imported fruit be sprayed with pesticides to prevent insects or diseases from reaching domestic crops. They sprayed the hold of a fruit ship arriving from the Ivory Coast in Africa just before it docked in Brazil. They subsequently found the bodies of 10 stowaways who had hidden in the ship's hold and who had been poisoned by the pesticides.

The Letter Left Out

The letter W is left out because it can always be written as UU—double U!

Lit Too Well?

During the blitz in World War II, London was subjected to heavy bombing by German planes. Sussex is south of London. It is on the flight path from Germany and part of its coastline resembles the Thames estuary. The authorities put lights in fields and in empty countryside to look like blacked-out London from the air. Some German aircrews were deceived and dropped their bombs in the wrong place.

Love Letters

She was a divorce lawyer drumming up business!

Message Received

Alexander the Great had the envoy's head shaved and then the message was tattooed on the envoy's head. Then he let the man's hair grow for a few weeks. When the envoy arrived, his head was shaved to reveal the message.

The Mighty Stone

The peasant first suggested putting props around the boulder to stabilize it. Then a team of workers dug a big hole around and halfway under the boulder. When the hole was big enough, they pulled away the props and the boulder rolled into the hole where it was then covered with earth.

Miscarriage of Justice

The Italian was Pontius Pilate, who released Barabbas and condemned Jesus Christ to die by crucifixion at Easter time. Every year Easter is marked by the sale of millions of chocolate Easter eggs worldwide.

The Mover

The letter t.

New World Record

The woman's great-great-granddaughter gave birth, so the old woman became the only known great-great-great-grandmother alive. The family had six generations alive at the same time.

No Charge

The man was totally deaf, so he did not hear his rights being read to him by the arresting officer.

Offenses Down

The police officers filled in their reports and forms while sitting in marked police cars parked outside the homes of known criminals. Drug dealers, fences, and burglars found it very inhibiting and bad for business to have a marked police car outside their houses. So crime went down.

The Old Crooner

The owners of shopping malls found that if they used Bing Crosby songs for the music in the public areas, then they had fewer undesirable youngsters hanging around and less crime was committed.

The Parson's Pup

The vicar wears black suits and knows that light-colored dog hairs will show up on his suits, but that black ones will not be noticed.

Peak Performance

In the climber's knapsack was his national flag, which he would have planted on the summit had he reached it.

Penalty

It was the women's World Cup and the match was played in a country with strict rules about female nudity or undressing in public.

Pesky Escalator

The foreign visitor saw a sign saying, "Dogs must be carried." He did not have a dog!

Poles Apart

Before the expedition the explorers deliberately ate a lot of fatty foods and put on several pounds of extra weight so that the fat would serve as food and fuel.

Police Chase

The getaway vehicle was a double-decker bus that went under a low bridge. The top deck of the bus was cut off and fell onto the pursuing police car. (This is a famous scene in a movie featuring James Bond, Agent 007.)

Pond Life

Because silk hats came into fashion, the demand for beaver hats decreased. More beavers meant more small lakes and bogs.

Poor Investment

The house was in a beautiful clifftop location. But within a few years, coastal erosion accelerated, and nothing could stop the house from eventually falling into the sea.

Poor Show

His name was Dick Fosbury, inventor of the famous Fosbury flop, a new high-jumping technique that involved going over the bar backward and that revolutionized the sport. He won the gold medal in the Mexico City Olympics in 1968.

Psychic

You notice that the woman is carrying a kettle. It is a very cold morning and only one of the cars has the windshield de-iced. You deduce correctly that she has defrosted her windshield with the kettle and is returning it to her home before setting off on her journey.

Quick on the Draw

The man's wife had played a trick on him. She called him to watch the drawing on TV and he was unaware that he was watching a video of the previous week's draw. She had bought him a ticket for today's draw and chosen the previous week's winning numbers.

Razor Attack

The woman forgot to plug in the razor!

Recognition

His Aunt Mary and his mother were identical twins.

Riotous Assembly

The institution was a university. Rioting students had raided the geology department and used rock samples as ammunition.

The Sad Samaritan

Jim found the full gas can in the trunk of his car. He had driven off and left the motorist stranded.

Scaled Down

The butcher had only one turkey left. The customer asked him its weight and he weighed it. The customer then asked if he had a slightly heavier one, so the butcher put the turkey away and then brought it out again. This time when he weighed it, he pressed down on the scale with his thumb in order to give it an exaggerated weight. The customer then said, "Fine—I'll take both!"

Sex Discrimination

It was found that the female lawyers wore underwire bras, which set off the very sensitive metal detectors.

Shakespeare's Blunder

The identical twins Viola and Sebastian are different sexes. This is impossible.

Shoe Shop Shuffle

One shop puts left shoes outside as samples; the other three shops put right shoes out. Display shoes are stolen, but the thieves have to form pairs, so more are taken from the store showing left shoes.

Shot Dead

The woman was a Russian sniper who, during the siege of Stalingrad in World War II, shot several German soldiers.

Siege Mentality

Several of the attacking soldiers had died of the plague. Their bodies were catapulted over the walls, and they infected many of the defenders, who were in a much more confined space. The defenders soon surrendered.

Sitting Ducks

The woman is an aeronautics engineer. She uses the gun to shoots ducks at airplane engines to test how they handle high-speed impacts with birds.

Slow Death

Aeschylus was killed when the tortoise was dropped on him from a height by an eagle who may have mistaken the bald head of Aeschylus for a rock on which to break the tortoise.

Sports Mad

The man wanted to record his favorite football team on TV. However, the safety tab on his only videocassette had been removed and he needed to cover the space with tape.

Stone Me!

David slew Goliath with a stone from his sling and a major battle was averted.

Strange Behavior

The man saw a tree lying across the road. He was in Africa and he knew that blocking the road with a tree was a favorite trick of armed bandits, who then waited for a car to stop at the tree so that they could ambush and rob the passengers. He guessed correctly that this was the case here, so he reversed quickly to avoid danger.

Take a Fence

The man had made green paint by mixing yellow paint and blue paint. The blue paint was oil-based, but the yellow paint was water-based. Heavy rain had dissolved the yellow paint, leaving the fence decidedly blue.

The Tallest Tree

The men chopped down the tree and then measured it on the ground!

Titanic Proportions

One of the reasons why so many perished on the Titanic was the shortage of lifeboats. Laws were passed to ensure that all ships had adequate lifeboats for all crew and passengers. One small ship took on so many lifeboats that it sank under their weight. (It must have been overloaded already!)

Tree Trouble

The foundation of the wall cut through the roots of the ancient tree and killed it.

Trunk-ated

A policeman suspects that there is the body of a murdered man in the trunk. He dials the cell phone of the victim and the phone is heard ringing in the trunk.

Two Heads Are Better Than One!

They were Native Americans who saw a European riding a horse. It was the first time they had seen a horse.

Two Letters

The man is given the world's most difficult crossword and offered a prize of $100 for every letter he gets right. He puts "S" for each initial letter and "E" in every other space. S is the commonest initial letter and E the commonest letter in the English language.

Unhealthy Lifestyle

The man was a heavy smoker. His smoke kept away mosquitoes and other insects. The woman died from an insect bite.

The Unwelcome Guest

The couple gave the neighbor a good meal, and when he finished, they gave his scrap-filled plate to the dog, who proceeded to lick it clean. They then put the plate straight back into the cupboard—pretending that was their normal procedure. The neighbor did not come back for any more meals!

Vandal Scandal

The authorities arranged for some chips of marble from the same original quarry source as the Parthenon to be distributed around the site every day. Tourists thought that they had picked up a piece of the original columns and were satisfied.

Watch That Man!

A picture of the runner early in the race showed him wearing his watch on his right wrist. When he crossed the finishing line, it was on his left wrist. The judges investigated further and found that one man had run the first half of the race and his identical twin brother had run the second half. They had switched at a toilet on the route.

Weight Loss

The doctor running the clinic had noticed that people living at high altitudes were generally thin. The air is thinner and people use more energy in all activities, including breathing. He therefore located his diet clinic at 8,000 feet above sea level and the patients found that they lost weight.

Well Trained

The child was correct. It was a mail train!

Wonderful Walk

During his walk in the woods, the man picked up several burrs on his clothes. When he returned home, he examined them under his microscope and discovered the mechanism whereby they stick on. He went on to invent Velcro.

The World's Most Expensive Car

The most expensive car was the moon buggy used by astronauts to explore the moon. It was left there. Although NASA would like to sell it, no one can retrieve it!

Would You Believe It?

The second person was underwater, so the block floated up. The third person was on a space station, where there was no gravity, so when the block was released it floated unsupported.

Wally Test Answers

Here are the answers to the WALLY Tests. Be prepared to groan!

Rate your score on the following scale:

Number Correct:	Rating:
8 to 10	WALLY Whiz
6 to 7	Smart Aleck
3 to 5	WALLY
0 to 2	Ultra-WALLY

WALLY Test 1

1. No. He will take his glass eye out of its socket and bite it.
2. No. He will take out his false teeth and bite his good eye with them.
3. You stand back to back.
4. The shadow of a horse.
5. Mr. Bigger's son. No matter how big Mr. Bigger is, his son is a little Bigger!
6. Tom's mother's third child was named Tom.
7. Egypt, Greenland, and Niagara Falls.
8. A glove.
9. An amoeba.
10. A blackboard.

WALLY Test 2

1. Snow.
2. Hide their shovels!
3. It was just a stage he was going through!
4. He was given the Nobel Prize.
5. Mickey Mouse.
6. He changed his name to Exit.
7. At a boxing arena.
8. A hare piece.
9. Don't feed him.
10. To get his feet in (all pants have three large holes).

WALLY Test 3

1. Your feet off the floor.
2. A ditch.
3. Albert. (He deferred to Queen Victoria's wish that no future king be called Albert.)
4. A walk!
5. There are 204 squares of varying sizes on a regular eight-by-eight chessboard.

6. 12—the second of January, the second of February, etc.

7. He throws it straight up.

8. Greenland. Australia is a continental landmass.

9. He does not have a door in his pajamas.

10. 5 minutes.

WALLY Test 4

1. ONE NEW WORD.

2. The letter N.

3. Neither—"Seven eights are 56."

4. They threw one cigarette away, thus making the boat a cigarette lighter.

5. 11 seconds. There are 11 intervals as opposed to 5.

6. Whoever the current U.S. president is. His name then was the same as it is today.

7. Tom Hanks and Carl Lewis.

8. No time—you can't have half a hole.

9. He broke out with measles!

10. You should stick in on the package, not on yourself!

WALLY Test 5

1. Because it has more geese in it!

2. Because they all have telephone lines!

3. So that he can fit in the small spaceship.

4. Exactly where you left him!

5. One. It takes many bricks to build the house but only one brick to complete it.

6. Take away his credit cards!

7. Edam is "made" backward.

8. A mailman.

9. Wet.

10. Take away their chairs.

WALLY Test 6

1. Lemon-aid

2. A lid.

3. The lion.

4. His horse was called "yet."

5. Get someone else to break the shell.

6. Because he was dead.

7. They use rope.

8. If they lifted up that leg, they would fall over.

9. Wintertime.

10. It wooden go!

Critical Answers

Balance

First, use the balance to divide the 80 grams into two piles of 40 grams. Then divide one of the 40-gram piles in half. Now balance the 20 grams against the 7 grams produced by the two masses. The 13 grams that are removed from the balance form one pile. The 7 grams added to the 40 grams + 20 grams produces the larger pile of 67 grams.

Big Magic

The sum of the side is thirty-four, and the square looks like this:

1	11	6	16
8	14	3	9
15	5	12	2
10	4	13	7

Break It Up!

Nine toothpicks need to be removed as shown below.

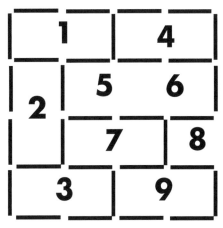

Breaking the Rules

Two inches. Each chalk piece will advance only half the distance covered by the ruler.

Breaking Up Is Hard to Do... Sometimes

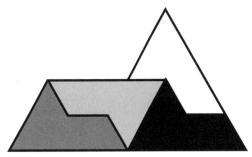

Bridge, Anyone?

The sticks below are arranged so that they support each other in a central triangle formed by over- and underlapping supports.

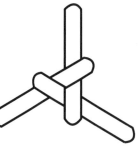

Cards, Anyone?

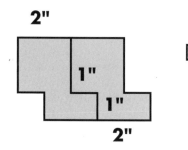
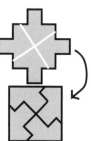

Change of Pace

a. either 5 pennies ($.05) + 4 nickels ($.20)

   + 1 quarter ($.25) = $.50; or 10 nickels ($.05) = $.50

b. 25 pennies ($.25) + 1 nickel ($.05)

   + 2 dimes ($.20) + 2 quarters ($.50) = $1.00

Check It Out

		4		
	1		2	
	5			
				3
6				

A Class Act

Seven students play only keyboards. A diagram helps illustrate and solve this problem.

Coin Roll

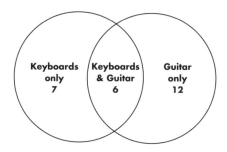

The coins maintain their relative position to each other as they move along the track. What changes is the direction in which the coin images point.

Cool Cut

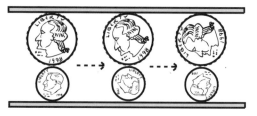

278

Make the cut from one corner straight across to the corners as shown below. Each side of this regular triangle that is formed is equal in length to the diagonal of the square.

Doing Wheelies

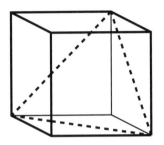

Wheel A would be spinning at five revolutions per minute. Wheel B would be spinning at twenty revolutions per minute. The difference in speed results from the "gearing up" and the "gearing down" from the first wheel set to the second wheel set. The belts between the second and third wheel sets do not affect the spin.

Don't Stop Now

Exactly... Well, Almost

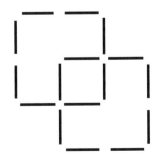

E. It is the mirror image of the other repeating (but rotating) design.

Face Lift

a. Eighteen faces.

b. Twenty-six faces.

c. Twenty-two faces.

A Game for Losers

By placing your "O" marker in either of the boxes indicated below, you are ensured a victory no matter where your opponent places his or her "X"s.

Get Set. Go!

150 miles long. In order to complete 30 miles of distance, the faster cyclist requires 1 hour of time while the slower cyclist needs 1.20 hours. Therefore, the time difference per 30 miles of travel is .20 hours. In order to increase the difference to 1 hour, multiple the 30 miles by 5.

Give Me Five

IIII. Easy, unless of course you forget all it takes to solve this problem is to divide 5555 by 5!

Going Batty

The number of beetles captured on each successive night were 8, 14, 20, 26, and 32.

Good Guess

Forty-eight gumballs. Since two guesses were off by seven and no guesses were repeated, these values had to refer to numbers at the opposite extremes of the spread. The two extremes are 41 and 55. If you add 7 to one and take 7 away from the other, you arrive at the middle number of 48.

Here, Art, Art, Art

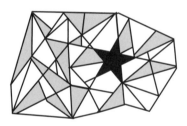

Here, Spot, Spot, Spot

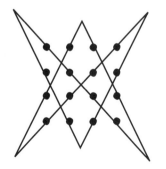

Iron Horse Race

The trains will be tied 3 hours after the faster train (or $4^1/2$ hours after the slower train) begins the race. For example, if the trains travel 60 mph and 90 mph, the $4^1/2$-hour journey for the slower train covers 270 miles, while the 3-hour journey for the faster train also covers 270 miles.

Keep On Tickin'

First you'll need to find out what each section needs to add to. To get this number, add up every number on the clock's face ($1 + 2 + 3 + 4 + 5 + 6 + 7 + 8 + 9 + 10 + 11 + 12 = 78$). Divide 78 by 3 and you'll get 26—the sum that each section must add to. The next part is relatively easy, since the numbers are already laid out in a ready-to-add pattern.

Keeping Time

Six hours. In 6 hours, the slow clock will be exactly 30 minutes behind while the fast clock will be exactly 30 minutes ahead of time.

Lasagna Cut

Each person gets one large and one small triangular piece.

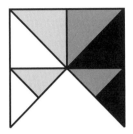

Here's a slightly different pattern that produces four similar-shaped slices (if we assume the connecting points between the triangle pairs remain uncut).

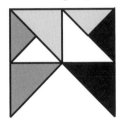

Look Over Here

The direction of the look is based upon the number of neighboring eyes that are in contact with the eye's circumference. Eyes that "touch" three other circles (such as the circle in question) have a pupil that points to the right.

Magic Star

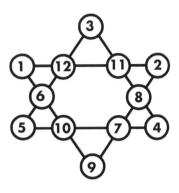

Main Attraction

Take either bar (it doesn't matter which one) and touch one end of the bar to the middle of the other bar. If the bar you are holding is a magnet, then its pole will cause the nonmagnetized bar to move. If, however, you've picked up the nonmagnetized bar, no attraction will occur. That's because neither of the poles is being touched.

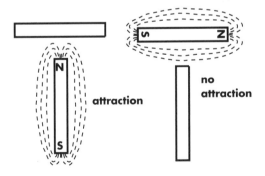

Melt Down

The level of water will not change. Although the top of the cube floats above the surface of the water, the amount of water in the entire ice cube can fill a space equal to the dimensions occupied by the part of the cube that is under the water's surface. In other words, as the ice cube turns to water, it produces the same amount of water as the space occupied by the submerged part of the cube.

Mind Bend

Place three parallel cuts in the card. Two of the cuts should be positioned on one side, while a single central cut should be made on the opposite side (as shown below). Then place a twist in the card so that half of the upper surface is formed by the "bottom-side" of the card. For extra fun, you might want to tape the folded card by all of its edges to the desk (making it more difficult to uncover the baffling "twist").

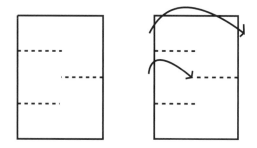

More Cheese

No. Six cuts are the fewest number of cuts needed to produce the twenty-seven smaller cubes. Stacking doesn't result in fewer cuts. Think of it this way: that innermost cube of the twenty-seven must be formed by a cut on each of its six sides.

Mind Slice

The angle of the cut will not affect the shape at all. All cuts will produce faces that are perfect circles. The feature that does change with the cutting angle is the circle size.

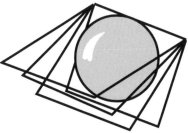

More Coinage

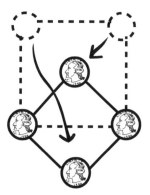

More Wheelies

480 revolutions. Since wheel B's rim is four times longer than wheel A's rim, it spins at one-fourth the speed (4 rps). Likewise, wheel B's rim is twice as long as wheel C's rim. Therefore, wheel C's rim spins twice as fast (8 rps). In 1 minute, C wheel will complete 60 x 8 revolutions, or 480 revolutions.

Number Blocks

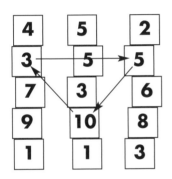

One Way Only

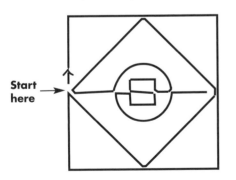

Parts of a Whole

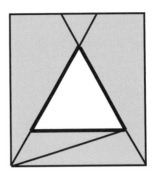

Puzzle Paths

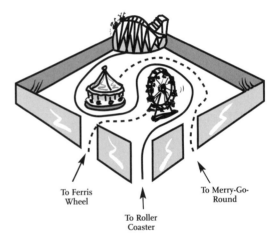

Oops, I Wasn't Concentrating

It is weaker than the original solution. In order have the original concentration, Anthony would have to add grape juice that is $2\frac{1}{2}$ times the regular strength.

Raises and Cuts

They are now both earning the exact same amount. To prove this, let's take a sample first-week salary of $100 for both Moe and

Bo. After the first adjustment, Moe earned $110 while Bo earned $90. During the second adjustment, Moe was cut by $11 to $99. At the same time, Bo was increased by $9 to $99.

Runaway Runway

Six intersections as shown below.

Roller Coaster Roll

Young Ed. The car that travels along the curved slope accelerates faster. This extra speed results from the quick drop in the path that allows the car to quickly pick up speed as the car moving down the straight slope accelerates at a slower and more uniform rate.

Satellite Surveyor

80 square miles. If you examine the dissected grid, you'll uncover that the composite shapes include side-by-side pairs that can be joined to form four squares. The total area is 20 X 20, or 400 square miles. Each of the five identical squares contains one-fifth, or 80 square miles.

Say Cheese

Make three cuts that divide the cube into eight smaller but equal cubes. Each of these eight cubes has a side length of 1 inch to produce a surface area of 6 square inches. The sum of the eight cube surface areas is 48 square inches.

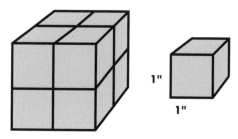

Screws in the Head

As the threads turn, they will produce a counterclockwise motion in the gear of the tuning post. This motion will decrease the tension in the string to produce a note of lower pitch.

Screwy Stuff

The threads of screw A form a spiral that would "go into" the wood block. In contrast, the opposite spiral of screw B would result in this screw moving out of the wooden block.

Separation Anxiety

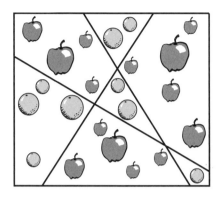

Sequence Grid

Triangle. The grid is filled by a series of number sequences. The first sequence consists of only one member—a square. The second and adjoining sequence includes a square + circle. The third sequence expands to include a square + circle + triangle. The complete sequence from which the "?" can be determined is square + circle + triangle + triangle + circle + circle.

Some Things Never Change

7 + 49 + 343 + 2401 + 16,807 = 19,607.

Spiral²

The complete path from entrance to center is 5000 feet. To obtain this distance, determine the total area of the structure (10,000 square feet). Now mentally unroll the spiral. Divide the 10,000-square-foot area by the area associated with one foot of forward travel. Since the corridor is 2 feet wide, the area for a single foot of forward motion is 2 square feet. Dividing 10,000 by 2, we arrive at the total distance of 5000 feet.

The Race Is On

The wheel with the centrally placed lead will accelerate fastest. This behavior reflects a property of physics that ice skaters execute during their moves. As a skater spins, the speed of the spin can be adjusted by altering his or her distribution of weight. As the arms extend, the spinning skater slows. As the arms draw in, the spin accelerates.

Sum Puzzle

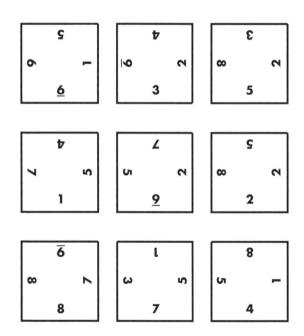

Surrounded By Squares

Thirteen squares.

Take 'em Away

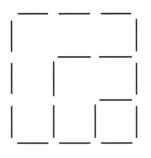

Take Your Pick

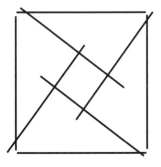

Thick as a Brick

Sixty bricks. You don't have to count all of the bricks. Just count the bricks in the uppermost layer (twelve) and multiply by the number of layers (five) so that you arrive at a total number of sixty bricks.

Time on Your Hands

7:22. For each given time, the minute hand advances a quarter of a complete counterclockwise rotation, while the hour hand advances three-eighths of a complete counterclockwise rotation. The final arrangement looks like this:

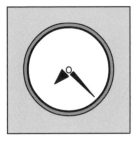

Togetherness

The computer weighs 16 pounds and its monitor weighs 32 pounds.

Trying Times

Eight unique triangles as shown below.

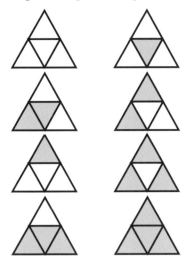

Turn, Turn, Turn

F.

Weighty Problem

120 pounds. If she needs to add "half of her weight" to get her full weight, then the weight that she does tell (60 pounds) must be half of her total. Therefore, 60 pounds is half of her weight. 60 + 60 = 120 pounds. If this doesn't seem right, just work it backwards starting with the 120 pounds.

What's the Angle?

a. Three copies of this shape are positioned as shown here.

Whale of a Problem

Two minutes. The amount of time needed to catch the seals doesn't change. Since two whales can catch two seals in 2 minutes, it is logical to assume that a single whale can catch one seal in that same period of time. Likewise, three whales can catch three seals in 2 minutes. As long as the number of whales is equal to the number of seals, the time doesn't change. Therefore, ten killer whales will also take 2 minutes to catch ten seals.

Wrap It Up

d. Here's what you see as you unwrap the folds.

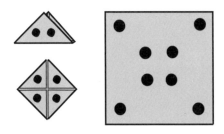

Pyramid Passage

Magic Pyramid

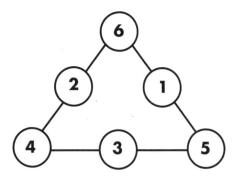

Pyramid Builders

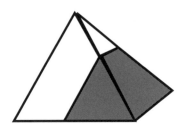

Trial by Triangle

1. In order to create these four equal triangles, you'll have to use all three dimensions. By constructing a three-dimensional pyramid shape, you'll create same-sized triangles on the structure's three sides and bottom.

2. Like the impossible triangle, these two objects are optical illusions and cannot be built.

Trapezoids 2 Triangle

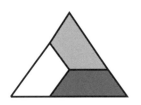

Spare My Brain

Since the four wheels share the journey equally, simply divide 50,000 by four and you'll get 12,500 miles per tire.

Whirling Paradox

Relative to a stationary observer, the top of the wheel is moving faster than the bottom of the wheel. It all has to do with the forward motion of the car. Since the top half of the wheel is moving in the same direction as the car, their speeds are added together to obtain the relative speed of the moving upper spoke.

However, the lower spokes are moving in the opposite direction as the car. In this case, subtraction of the speeds results in a much slower relative speed—slow enough to count the individual spokes.

Lost?

To find out which way to go, you need to stand the sign back up.

Since you came from Skullara, align the sign so that the Skullara arrow points back to it. All the other arrows will then be pointed to the correct directions.

Sand Traps

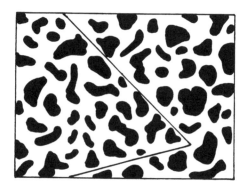

Which Mountain?

It doesn't matter which mountain you climb. All three paths will be the same length. The length of the path is not determined by the shape of the mountain but the slope of the road.

Since all three mountain paths have the same slope, you'd have to walk the same distance in order to climb each 10,000 foot summit.

Compass Caper

White. The bear must be a polar bear. To conform to the given pattern, the hiker must begin the trek at the magnetic North Pole.

A Cut Above

Make two cuts to divide the pizza along its diameter into four equal parts. Then stack the quarters on top of each other. Make another cut down the middle of the stack.

Although it might be messy, you'll have eight equal slices.

Kitchen Cups

Fill the three-cup container with water. Pour it into the five-cup container. Fill the three-cup container again, and fill up the five-cup container. This will leave you with exactly one cup of water in the three-cup container.

Moldly Math

This is simpler than it may seem. Since the mold doubles in size every day, it covered half as much area one day before!

And a Cut Below

Eight pieces as shown below:

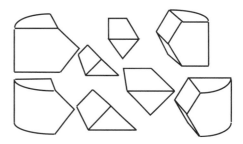

Egg Exactly

Simultaneously turn over the five and three minute timers when you begin to boil the water.

When the three minute timer runs out, put the egg into the boiling water. When the five minute timer runs out, the egg is done. Two minutes have elapsed.

Losing Marbles?

Start spinning the marble along the bottom of the cup so that it pushes against the inner wall.

When the spin is fast enough, the force overcomes the pull of gravity and the cup can be turned upside down.

A Puzzle of Portions

There are several ways to divide the juice. Here's one of the quickest:

Vessel size	24	13	11	5
To start	24	0	0	0
First	8	0	11	5
Second	8	13	3	0
Third	8	8	3	5
Fourth	8	8	8	0

Mixed Up?

There is the same amount of root beer in the cola as there is cola in the root beer.

For every drop of root beer that is in the cola cup, a drop of cola has been displaced and is in the root beer cup.

Toothpick Teasers

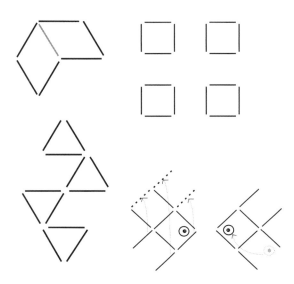

Going to the Movies

Tracing, counting, and remembering each step would drive you crazy. To make things easier, just write down the possible paths to each circle. The number of paths to the next circle is equal to the sum of the paths that connect to it.

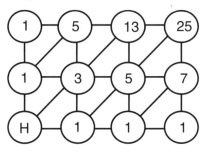

Now Seating?

1. There are ten possible combinations: BBGGG, BGBGG, BGGBG, BGGGB, GBBGG, GBGBG, GBGGB, GGBBG, GGBGB, GGGBB.

2. The chances for two boys being on the ends are 1 in 10.

3. The chances for two girls being on the ends are 3 in 10.

Weighing In...

The weight of the jar doesn't change. In order to fly, the insects must produce downward air currents that are equal in force to their weight. Therefore, whether standing or in flight, the insects push down with the same force.

The Strangest Eyes

Unfortunately, you will need to check this one by tracing over the pattern. As you do, you'll discover a single loop on the left and a double loop on the right.

Monkey Business

Both the crate and the chimp go up.

Head Count

Although this type of problem is perfect for algebra, let's do it visually. If all of the thirty heads belonged to two-legged birds, then there'd be only sixty legs. If one of the animals has four legs, then there'd be sixty-two legs. If two animals are four-legged, there'd be sixty-four legs.

By continuing in this pattern until we reach seventy legs, we will get a combination of twenty-five birds and five lizards.

Möbius Strip

The shape you get from dividing the Möbius strip is one large continuous loop with four twists.

Ant Walk

Nine centimeters. One basic pattern is illustrated below. Although there are other turns, they cover the same total length.

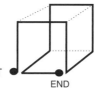

Cubic Quandaries

There is a total of 27 cubes. There are six cubes with one red side, twelve cubes with two red sides, eight cubes with three red sides, and one cube with no red sides.

Squaring Off

Saving Face

1. The face should have a circle design.

2. The pattern folds into a cube that looks like this:

3. Folding the creases would produce this final version:

D

Cut the Cards

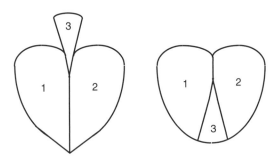

Stripped Stripe

Here is the cut pattern....

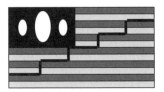

and here is the reassembly.

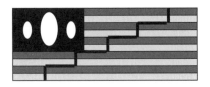

Missing Square

There isn't an extra block. The area making the new block was "shaved off" from some of the other blocks. The loss of each block's area is so small that it's not easy to observe.

Tipping the Scales

Snake Spread

The snakes will fill their stomachs and not be able to swallow anymore. The circle will then stop getting smaller.

Falcon Flight

The falcon's total distance is determined by the amount of time he was aloft and the speed he maintained.

The speed is given. The time is derived from the two cyclists. Since the cyclists are 60 miles apart and drive towards each other at 30 mph, the total time elapsed is 2 hours. The bird flying at 45 miles per hour will cover 90 miles in this 2-hour period.

A Question of Balance

It has to do with friction, balance, and the weight of the yardstick.

As you move your fingers towards the middle of the yardstick, the balance of the yardstick shifts. The finger that is closer to the middle will support more weight, making it easier for the other, more distant finger to "catch up" and move closer to the middle as well. This "catching up" flip-flops between the two fingers until they both arrive at the middle of the yardstick.

The finger that moves first from the middle immediately bears less of the ruler's weight, which makes it easier for this finger to keep moving. The farther it moves, the easier sliding becomes.

Well-Balanced Plate

You must mirror your opponent's placement of the plate. This way, as long as he has a place for his plate, you have a place for yours.

Robot Walkers

The robots follow a path that forms a continually shrinking and rotating square. Eventually, the robots will meet in the middle of the square.

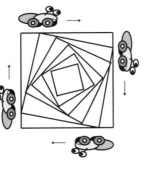

Chain Links

Select the chain with three links. Break open one of the links and use it to connect any two of the other sections. Break another of its links and use it to connect two other sections. Break the third and final link and use it to make a complete loop.

Rope Ruse

Fold your arms as shown above. Then, pick up the free end of the rope while your arms are already crossed. As you uncross your arms, the rope will automatically knot itself.

Money Magic

The clips will lock together and drop off the bill. A paper clip isn't a complete loop. It has two stretched openings through which the clip can slip off the bill. As the two sections of the bill move by each other, the clips slip through their openings and are pushed together to "reclip" onto each other's loop.

Revolutionary Thoughts

Four and a half hours. In order to be in a straight line the satellites must travel either one full revolution or one-half revolution. In $4^{1}/_{2}$ hours, they'll look like this:

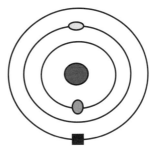

Baffling Holes

Fold the card in half so that the circular hole is also folded in half. Then slightly twist the paper as you pass the quarter snugly through the hole.

A Fair Solution

1. Either teenager can cut the slice, but the other person selects who gets which slice.

2. The four removed toothpicks leave the word "TEN."

Sock It to Me

Four socks. In a worst case scenario, if you draw three socks, each of a different color, the next sock you draw guarantees a matching color.

Nuts!

1. As you rotate each screw in a clockwise direction, they come together.

2. City-owned bulbs have opposite threads so that they won't screw into the standard light sockets that people have in their homes. Therefore, this discourages theft.

Doubtful Dimensions

A box with 3 x 4 dimensions has a diagonal length of 5 feet.

Machine Madness

Midway between 10 and 11 o'clock. The rotation decreases from one-quarter turn to one-eighth turn between the second and third wheel.

As the smaller hub of the second wheel rotates one-quarter turn, it moves the attached belt by only 1 foot. The 1-foot belt movement spins the larger third wheel only one-eighth of a revolution. This one-eighth turn remains the same for the fourth and fifth wheel. The belt twist between the first and second wheel changes the spin from clockwise to counterclockwise.

Putting It Together

The list contains fifty pairs of numbers that add to 100 (100+0, 99+1, 98+2, 97+3, etc.) with the number 50 as an unpaired leftover. 50   100 + 50 = 5,050.

The Heat Is On

As the washer expands, so does the hole it forms. Think of the washer as an image being stretched on a graphics program. Both the washer and its encircled hole will enlarge.

City Pipes

It is impossible for the round sewer cover to fall into the round pipe.

If the cover and tube had rectangular dimensions, the cover would be able to slip into the tube by being tilted in diagonally.

But no matter how you tilt the circular cover, it can't fit through a hole of the same dimension.

Magic Square

8	3	4
1	5	9
6	7	2

Anti-Magic Square

5	1	3
4	2	6
8	7	9

Numbers Game

The trick to figuring out the key number is to subtract the winning number by the next number after your range of playing numbers.

For instance, because you can only use the numbers 1–5, if you work in increments 6 down from 50, you will get your key numbers: 8, 14, 20, 26, 32, 38, 44.

What's Next?

The symbols are the mirror images of the numbers 1 to 4 rotated on their side. The next image is a 5, modified in the same way.

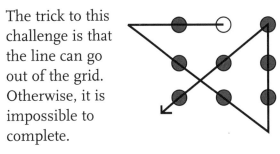

Connect the Dots

The trick to this challenge is that the line can go out of the grid. Otherwise, it is impossible to complete.

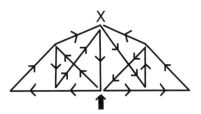

Another Ant Walk

In Order

1. Girl walks to right wearing raingear and umbrella, passes grocery store, in the heavy rain.

2. Girl walks to right, passes record store, wearing raingear and umbrella, in less rain.

3. Girl stops, umbrella up, she holds out

hand to feel rain. There is no rain.

4. Girl has stopped, folds up umbrella. There is no rain.

5. Girl walks to left, holds folded umbrella, passes record store. There is no rain.

6. Girl walks to left, holds folded umbrella, passes grocery store. There is no rain.

7. Girl walks to right holding baseball bat, passes grocery store. It is sunny.

8. Girl walks to right, passes record store, holds baseball bat. It is sunny.

Tangrams

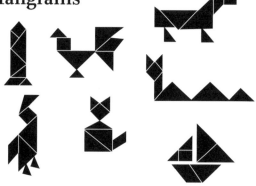

Fractured Farmland

Eighteen: one whole composite block (1,2,3,4,5,6); six separate blocks (1) (2) (3) (4) (5) (6); three horizontal pairs (1&4) (2&5) (3&6); four vertical pairs (1&2)

1	4
2	5
3	6

(2&3) (4&5) (5&6); two vertical triplets (1,2,3) (4,5,6); two large blocks (1,4,2&5) (2,5,3&6)

Number Sense

Three. Each number identifies the numbers of overlapping rectangles that cover that space.

What Comes Next?

D. During each step, the shades advance according to the following rule.

The Marked Park

Sixty-three feet. The lowest common denominator between the small wheel (7 feet) and large wheel (9 feet) is obtained by multiplying seven and nine.

Pattern Path

The sequence of the path is made by multiplying the digits by two: 2,4,8,16,32,64,128, etc. Here's a small part of that path:

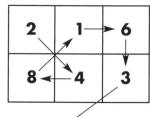

Pile Puzzler

To make things easy, first find the total value for each pile by adding up all the card values. Divide the sum (forty-five) by three to get the value for each pile (fifteen).

Pattern Puzzler

Three. The central number (E) is obtained by dividing the product of the top (A) and bottom (B) numbers by the product of the right (D) and left (C) numbers. A x B/C x D = E.

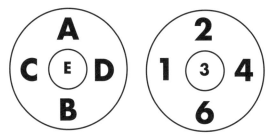

Titillating Tiles

54/22. With the other tiles, when you multiply the individual digits of the top number, you arrive at the bottom number. For example: 4 x 8 = 32.

Pattern Grid

D. The grid is divided into four 4 x 4 tiles. As you go in a "Z" pattern from the top left tile to right to bottom left to right, you'll see that the tile rotates one-quarter turn.

Brain Net

Twenty routes. Although you can chart them all out, there is a less confusing way. Starting at the left, identify the number of routes that can get you to a circle. You can arrive at this number by adding the numbers found in the connecting cir-cles to the left. Keep going until you get to the finish.

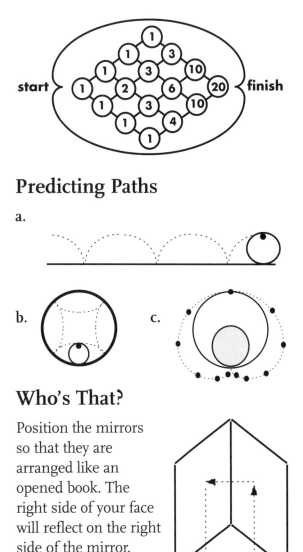

Predicting Paths

a.

b.

c.

Who's That?

Position the mirrors so that they are arranged like an opened book. The right side of your face will reflect on the right side of the mirror. This image does not reflect back to that eye. Instead, it bounces to the other mirror. From there, the image is reflected back to the other eye.

Leftovers Again?

Thirty-one statues. The 25 ounces are used directly to make twenty-five statues. During this process, 5 ounces of excess clay are produced. This extra clay is used to make five additional statues. While making these five additional statues, there is enough unused clay to make one more statue with one-fifth of the clay left over.

Brownie Cut

One cut

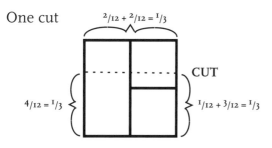

Balancing Gold

Nine pounds. Examine the objects on the right side of the balance. If we looked at the balance pan containing the two bars, we'd see that one-tenth of the gold bar is absent. In its place we have nine-tenths of a pound. From this we can infer that one-tenth of a gold bar weighs nine-tenths of a pound. Therefore, a complete gold bar would weigh ten times as much. 9/10 pound 10 = 90/10, or 9 pounds.

Thrifty Technique

First, divide the coins into three groups of three. Then, balance any one group against another group. If the counterfeit is contained in either of the groups, the coins will not balance. If, however, they balance, the counterfeit coin must be in the third pile. Now that we have identified the pile with the counterfeit coin, remove one coin from the pile and balance the other two. The lighter coin will not balance. If the two coins do balance, the counterfeit coin is the one not selected.

Tricky Tide

Five rungs will still remain exposed. As the tide comes in, the boat will rise up.

Breaking Up Is Hard to Do

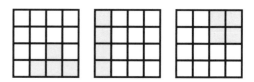

Disorder

	7	
3	1	4
5	8	6
	2	

True or False?

Tarsal. To figure this one out, we need to look at each alien's response. If the first alien was a tarsal, it would identify itself as a tarsal. If it was a carpal, it would still identify itself as a tarsal. Either way, the mumbling alien would identify itself as a "tarsal." Therefore, the second alien had to be lying. The third alien truthfully identified the carpal, making him a truth-telling tarsal.

Pack Up Your Troubles

The "trick" is using the same block in the rows of two adjacent sides.

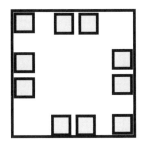

Don't Come Back This Way Again!

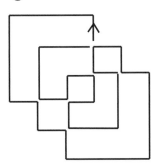

Meet Me on the Edge

One in six. The ant (or fly) can take any one of the six available routes. It doesn't matter.

Now, the other insect must select the "collision route" from its own six possible choices. Therefore, the odds are one in six.

Only the Shadow Knows?

They can never cast shadows of equal size.

Any difference in their altitude would be negligible compared to their distance to the sun. It's those 93,000,000 miles from our planet to the sun that affect the shadows' size much more than their puny distances apart.

More Shadow Stuff

At that time of day, the shadow is two-fifths of the object's height. If the tree's shadow (two-fifths of the unknown height) is 25 feet, then the height of the tree is $62\frac{1}{2}$ feet.

Trip Times

Since it takes her 1 hour to reach the top (while traveling at 30 mph), the hill is a 30-mile route. Traveling at 60 mph, she'll cover that distance in only 30 minutes.

The average speed is the total distance/total time = 60 miles/1.5 hours or 40 mph.

Average Puzzle

There is no way that she can average 20 mph for the whole trip. Like the uphill path, the downhill path is only 10 miles. This distance is too short to achieve an average speed (for the whole trip) of 20 mph.

Consider this: If she completed her trip by traveling the downhill path at 600 mph, then her average speed would be the total distance divided by the total time, or 20 miles/61 minutes, or an average of about 19.6 mph.

By examining this equation, you'll see that there will be no way for her to decrease the denominator (time) below the 60 minutes she has already spent cycling up the hill.

Palindrome

55 mph. The next palindrome that the odometer can display is 14,041. To reach this value, Bob will have had to travel 110 miles. If it took him 2 hours to reach this point, his average speed will be 55 mph.

All other palindromes would have required too many miles to produce a logical speed. For example, the odometer's next palindrome is 14,141. From this, you can calculate an average speed of 105 mph—highly unlikely.

Stacking Up

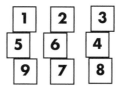 or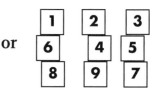

Star Birth

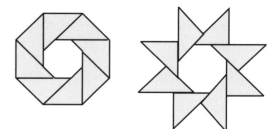

Flip Flop

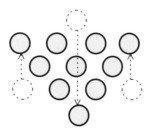

Crossing Hands

Eleven times. For each hour up until 11:00, the clock's hands will cross once. Between 11 am and 1 pm, they'll only cross once (at noon). For each remaining hour between 1 pm and 5 pm, the clock's hands will cross once. That gives us a total of 6 + 1 + 4 = 11 times.

What's Next?

The sequence is based on the expanding geometric figures. After each figure reaches the outside perimeter, it starts again at the center.

Trying Triangles

Thirty-five triangles.

Flipping Pairs

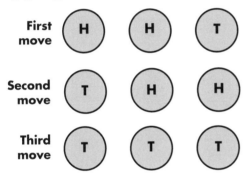

Missing Blocks

a. Twenty-three blocks. None are missing from the bottom layer, six are missing from the second layer, eight are missing from the third layer, and nine are missing from the top layer.

b. Seventeen blocks. Eight are hidden in the bottom layer, six are hidden in the second layer, three are hidden in the third layer, and none are hidden in the top layer.

Matchstick Memories

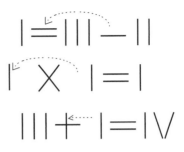

Sum Circle

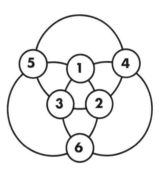

Many Rivers to Cross

First, the two children row to the far side. There, one gets out. The other child returns and gives the boat to an adult. The adult crosses the river. On the far side, the adult gets out and the child gets in the boat. The child brings the boat across the river and transports the other child back to the far side. This pattern continues until the four adults have crossed.

Train Travel

15 minutes and 32 seconds. This problem is not as simple as it may appear. The distance from pole one to pole ten is nine

units. As stated, it takes the train 10 minutes to travel this distance. Therefore, it takes the train 1 minute and one-ninth (about 6.6 seconds) to travel each inter-pole distance.

From the first pole to the fifteenth pole is fourteen inter-pole distances. It should take 14 x 1 minute and 6.6 seconds, or 14 minutes and 92 seconds, or about 15 minutes and 32 seconds.

Miles Apart

120 miles. This problem is full of extra (and unneeded) information.

Think it backwards. One hour before they meet, one train is 65 miles away from the meeting point, while the other is 55 miles. Add the two distances together and you'll get 120 miles.

Passing Trains

792 feet. The length of the freight train can be calculated by knowing its relative passing speed and the time it took for it to move by. The passing speed is equal to the sum of both train speeds (60 mph +30 mph = 90 mph).

Here's where some conversion comes in. By dividing by sixty, we find that 90 mph is equal to 1.5 miles per minute. By dividing by sixty again, we find that this is equivalent to 0.025 miles per second.

The freight train takes 6 seconds to pass. Therefore, its length is 0.15 miles. To change this into feet, multiply 0.15 by the number of feet in a miles (5,280).

Souped-Up Survey

The numbers do not add up correctly. The agency stated that only one hundred people were interviewed. Yet, according to a logical breakdown of the results, they received 120 responses. You can see by making a diagram of the data.

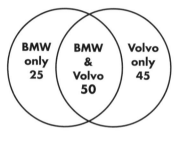

Toasty

Fry one side of two slices for 30 seconds. Flip one slice over and replace the other slice with a fresh slice of bread. At the end of 1 minute, remove the completely fried bread. Return the unfried side of the previous slice to the pan and flip the other slice over for 30 seconds.

Circle Game

When added together, the numbers at the opposite ends of this sequence equal ten (1 + 9, 2 + 8, etc.). By placing a five in the middle circle, we ensure that all the sums must equal fifteen (10 + 5).

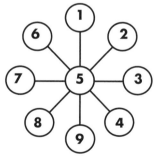

A Fare Split

$12.50. One-fourth of the total round trip fare ($5.00) was taken by Michelle alone. Three-fourths of the round trip was shared (half of $15.00). Therefore, Michelle should pay $5.00 + $7.50 or $12.50.

Pentagon Parts

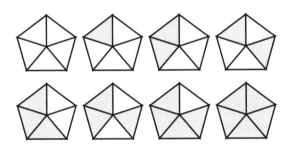

Bagel for Five?

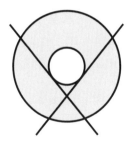

Coin Moves

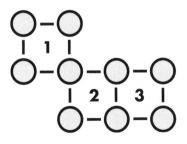

Trapezoid Trap

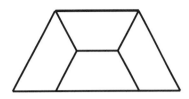

A+ Test

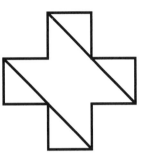

Mis-Marked Music

Select the box labeled "Rap & Jazz." Listen to one tape. If the marble is jazz, then you must have the box full of jazz cassettes. (Remember that since all the boxes are mislabeled, this box could not contain the mix of rap and jazz.) Likewise, if the tape is rap, you have selected the all-rap box. Since all three names are mismatched, then just switch the names of the other two boxes to correctly identify the contents of all boxes.

Measuring Mug

Fill the mug about two-thirds full of water. Then tilt it so that water pours off. When the level of water reaches the same height as the uplifted mug bottom, the vessel is then half full.

Coin Roll

a. The same direction—to the left.

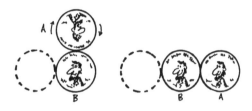

b. Two.

Painting on the Side

Ten ways. I = all sides white, I = one red face, I = two adjacent red faces, I = two opposite sides red faces, I = three sides red (in line), I = three faces red (in right-hand and left-hand L-shape design), I = four faces red (in line), I = four faces red (two pairs of two in line), I = five red faces, I = all faces red.

Magic Triangle

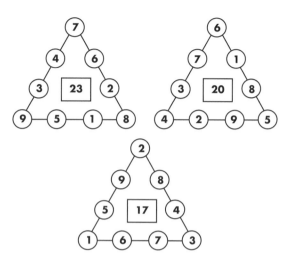

Patterns

Fourteen. Add the upper left number, lower left number, and lower right number together. Then multiply this sum by the number in the upper right corner. The product is in the center of the square.

Frog Jump

Four days. During the first day, the frog jumps up 6 feet and at night slides down 2 feet. The frog begins day two at a height of 4 feet, jumps to 10 feet, but slides back to 8 feet. On day three, the frog jumps to 14 feet, but slides back to 12 feet. On day four, the frog jumps to 18 feet and leaves the well.

Army Ants

Yes. Here's how.

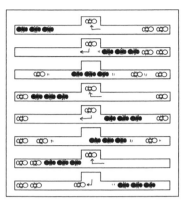

No Sweat

Five girls and two boys. First, subtract the coach's 9 cups from the total amount. Therefore, the boys and the girls together drank 34 cups. The winning combination is five girls (who together drink 20 cups) and two boys (who together drink 14 cups). 20 + 14 = 34 cups.

Go Figure!

Statement 4. The confusing relationship may best be understood by putting the information in a graphic layout. From the drawing, you can see that only statement 4 is true.

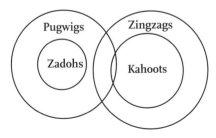

Square Pattern

There are only three distinguishing patterns. All other patterns are obtained by rotating the square.

r	g	b
b	r	g
g	b	r

b	g	r
r	b	g
g	r	b

g	r	b
b	g	r
r	b	g

Bouncing Ball

Approximately 3 meters. The first fall is 1 meter. It rebounds to $1/2$ meter, than falls fi meter. So now we're at 2 meters. Then the ball goes up and down $1/4$ meter, then $1/8$ meter, then $1/16$ meter, and so on. It continues this pattern until it comes to rest (theoretically it would keep going, but in the real world it stops). If we were to add all of these distances up, we'd get: $1 + 1/2 + 1/2 + 1/4 + 1/4 + 1/8 + 1/8 + 1/16 + 1/16 + ... = {\sim}3$ meters.

Complete the Pattern

X = 22; Y = 25. Each circle equals 1, each square equals 5, each triangle equals 10, and the pentagon equals 2. The numbers represent the sums of the values in each row or column.

Checkerboard

Thirty squares.

Cutting Edge

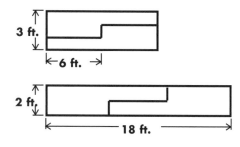

The Die Is Cast

Although all four dice have the same relative orientation of spots, the three spots on the last die tilt from the lower left corner to the upper right corner.

When the other dice are rotated onto this position, their three spots tilt from the upper left to the lower right corner.

Playing with Matches?

Thirty-one matches. If one winner is to be found in thirty-two teams, then thirty-one teams must lose. Since each team can only lose once, the thirty-one losses result from thirty-one matches.

Competing Clicks

Anthony. The actual period is 1 second less than the time given. Emily completes ten clicks in 9 seconds. Buzzy completes twenty clicks in 19 seconds. Anthony completes five clicks in 4 seconds. This gives us the approximate rates: Emily = 1.1 clicks/second, Buzzy = 1.05 clicks/second, Anthony = 1.25 clicks/second.

Another Pattern

Four. The number in the center of each triangle results from dividing the product of the top two sides by the bottom side.

Vive le Flag

Twenty-four combinations. If both of the outside stripes are the same color, you'll have twelve possible combinations (4 x 3 =12).

If all three stripes are a different color, you'll have twenty-four possible combinations (4 x 3 x 2 = 24). However, these twenty-four flags are made up of twelve mirror-image pairs. Just rotate the mirror image one-half turn and you'll produce the other flag. This decreases the stripe combinations to only twelve.

Now let's add the two sets of possible combinations: 12 + 12 = 24 different color patterns.

Pizza Cut

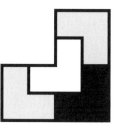

Slip Sliding

You'll get blocked if you don't place the coins in a specific order. Each coin must come to rest on the spot where the previous coin began its journey. Only in this manner can you then place all seven coins.

A, B, See?

10	55	919	545
x10	x55	x191	x455
100	110	1110	1000

Spare Change

$1.19. Jonathan has four pennies, four dimes, one quarter, one half dollar. Added together, they amount to $1.19.

Puzzling Prices

Ten dollars. The trick is not getting fooled into thinking that the book is five dollars.

If the book is "p," then $5 + 1/2p = p$.

$5 = 1/2p$.

$10 = p$.

Gum Drop

135 gum drops. If forty gum drops are left in the jar, the forty must represent two-thirds of the gum drops that were available when Britt appeared.

Therefore, the total number of gum drops before Britt took her share was sixty. Working with the same logic, you can figure out that before Tanya took her share of thirty, the jar had ninety gum drops. Before Michael took his share of forty-five, it had 135 gum drops.

Go-Cart Crossing

33.3 minutes. To travel 1 mile, go-cart A takes 1/6 of an hour, go-cart B takes 1/12 of an hour, and go-cart C takes 1/15 of an hour. To travel one loop distance (1/3 of a mile), it would take each 1/18, 1/36, and 1/45 of an hour, respectively. All three would meet at 1/9 of an hour intervals. For five meetings to occur, five 1/9-hour periods must pass. $5 \times 1/9 = 5/9$ of an hour, or about 33.3 minutes.

Table Manners

Two ways. White = female. Black = male.

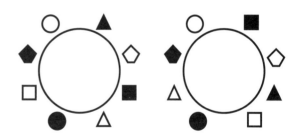

Winning Slip

The contestant picks one of the slips. The slip is placed out of view (possibly eaten). The contestant then asks the MC to read the slip that was not selected. That MC's slip has the word "loser." When the audience hears "loser," they logically conclude that the contestant must have picked the winning slip.

Ancient Man

60 years old. If his whole life is "X years," then:

His boyhood years = $\frac{1}{4}X$

His youth = $\frac{1}{5}X$

His adulthood = $\frac{1}{3}X$

His elder years = 13

$\frac{1}{4}X + \frac{1}{5}X + \frac{1}{3}X + 13 = X$

$X = 60$

Lights Out!

He covers the window as shown here, which meets both conditions.

Pencil Puzzle

V. The layout is based on the sequence of letters found in the alphabet. The "twist" is produced by the extra pencil points aimed at certain letters. Each pencil point can be replaced by the words "advance one step."

Look at the letter L (either one). The L progresses to M. The M, however, does not advance to an N because two M pencil points converge on this next space. The letter then advances one extra step, resulting in an O.

With the same logic, the O leads to an R (advance three steps). The R leads to a V (advance four steps).

Sounds Logical?

Niko. If Sheila picks rock 'n' roll, then according to (1) Ramon must pick jazz and according to (2) Niko must also pick jazz. These selections contradict (3). This rules Sheila out.

If Ramon picks jazz, then according to (1) Sheila must pick rock 'n' roll and the same contradictions surface.

The only person who can select either jazz or rock 'n' roll without any contradictions is Niko.

Triangular Tower

Twenty balls arranged in four levels.

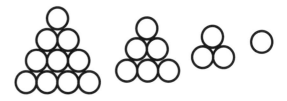

Criss-Crossed

Place one coin on top of the corner coin.

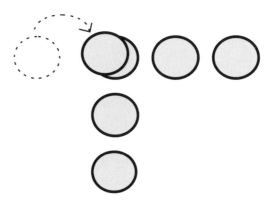

Crystal Building

Twelve tennis balls. Place six in a circle around the middle of the ball. Place three on top and three on the bottom.

Testy Target

Two arrows struck the 8 region (16 points) and seven of them struck the 12 region (84 points). Total: 16 + 84 = 100 points.

Eighth Century Enigma

On his first trip, the man brings the goat over (leaving the cabbage and wolf behind). On his second trip, he brings over the cabbage. When he lands on the other side, however, he takes the goat back in his boat. When he returns, he drops off the goat and takes the wolf. He transports the wolf across the river and leaves it with the cabbage. He returns once more to ferry over the goat.

Planet Rotation

The sun would now appear to rise in the west and set in the east. This change is caused by the switch in rotation spin. The switch in revolution does not affect the direction of the apparent sunrise or sunset.

Shuffle

The straight is more probable. To select the four of a kind, you need to select "one card out of five cards" four times: $1/5$ x $1/5$ x $1/5$ x $1/5$, or 1 out of 625.

For the straight, the first card can be any card. Then, you'll need to select "one card out of five cards" three times: $1/5$ x $1/5$ x $1/5$, or 1 out of 125—a better probability.

Some Exchange

a. 14 and 9. The sum of all eight numbers is sixty. Each column must have a sum equal to half that, or thirty. To arrive at thirty, you need to lessen one column by five and increase the other by the same amount. This is accomplished by exchanging a 14 for a 9.

b. 2, 1, and 3. As with the previous problem, you can add all nine numbers together, then divide that sum by three. The result is twenty:

7	2	1
3	6	2
10	12	17
20	20	20

Index